# COME TO THINK OF IT

## BY

# HERMINIA A. SISON

PRESS

# CONTENTS

# ACKNOWLEDGMENT

M y utmost thanks to the two persons who helped and supported me greatly in the preparation and publication of this book.

To Araceli Mathay, who among my friends, was the one who suggested to me, "Why don't you write a book?" With her encouragement, I thought about it, until I finally decided to do it.

And to Leonardo Jonson, my son-in-law, without whom this book would never have been published. He took charge of its publication—first, by preparing in manuscript form all of my hand-written chapters of the book. More importantly, he dealt personally with the publisher of his choice—the Xulon Press— particularly, with all those involved with my book's publication.

My special thanks to one of them—the illustrator, Natalie Marino. With her inspired, artistic illustrations, she added clarity and liveliness to the meanings, insights and symbols lodged in the contents of my book—both essays and narratives.

Dedicated to my children—Norman, Marissa, and Susan—who have always been the meaning, purpose, and happiness of my life.

And to the loving memory of my eldest daughter, Portia, who had been and always will be the inspiration in all my literary works.

And also, to my grandchildren and loved ones.

# Author's Note

I am writing this book in the pinnacle of age. I am ninety-one years old. Most probably, I am in the last decade of my years and life—and certainly true about anyone at such an age, for that matter.

You may ask, "Why wait that long to write it? Is there anything new or great about it?"

No, nothing new, nor great. But I hope something valuable. Otherwise, why write it at all? What's its purpose?

I am writing it to satisfy this nagging notion of mine that most of the lurking views and perspectives about life's realities arising from the grind of daily living elude one's mental grasp. It's especially more so because of the numerous vicissitudes confronting anyone in his day-to-day struggles against the onslaughts of time and fate that dull his sensitive awareness of the truth about himself arising from his relationship with others around him.

My sole and simple purpose in writing this book is to share my insights and thoughts about the commonplace realities surrounding everyone in this world of ours. More as a dramatist and playwright in my literary works, I am interested in the human drama taking place everywhere in the vast stage of life where everyone is a character with a part to play—however great or unnoticeable.

With my fresh attempt to go to other venues of writing, which I have done in this book, I put formal essay and narrative together with sprinkles of poetry and drama in them. It is my concept of a book's format—a kind of hodgepodge and combination of various areas of writing thrown together— essay, narrative, poetry, drama, and all—contained in every chapter. Adding to it all, I wrapped them with the rich resources in my mind's storehouse of memories gathered and culled from the personal stories, experiences, and adventures of my ninety-one years.

If you, my readers, while reading any chapter of my book, may pause momentarily, look up thoughtfully, and musingly say to yourself, "**Come to think of it**," then begin to ponder— that's when the purpose of my book is fulfilled.

To ponder is the essence and wealth of thought. And thinking is life itself.

# 1

# Image and Likeness

## Narrative: May the Better One Win

# Image and Likeness

W hat makes a person? What makes him unique and apart from any other person? The answer lies in his image and likeness blended together, which results in the appearance and personality that is his alone.

Yet, image and likeness are so dissimilar and different from each other, even poles apart in meaning and significance— and, therefore, cannot be easily blended together. They should be compared and seen separately.

How? Where lies the comparison? First of all, both words, "image" and "likeness," stem from one word, "sameness"— which is their origin in significance. If one's image is the replica of another, the sameness lies in their physical appearance. Whereas, the expression, "Like father, like son" no longer means physical appearance, but sameness in personality, attributes, and characters.

From another standpoint, image is visual and seen. Likeness is impression and felt. One is tangible, the other intangible. However, both words express "sameness." This applies not only to human beings, but also to other creatures and things as well. Therefore, it could be said that all in this world fall under one common category—the sameness in image and likeness with one another. This is a paradox, because it is in their sameness where their difference lies.

For instance, no two stones of the same matter can be perfectly alike in shape. Neither could two snowflakes be like each other. Nor two grains of sand in the seashore could be the exact match of each other. How much more with the highest creation of them all—the human being?

So, in essence, every created thing, animate or inanimate, is related to another—if not in likeness, then in image. But seldom, if ever at all, do the two go together to produce the uniqueness of a person—his appearance, character, personality, and all.

Man, in his religion, from the ancient past to the present, has always sought the answer to the paradox of image and likeness. Christians answered the question of image with the basic teaching of creation, whereby God created man in His own image. The ancient Greeks held the opposite view that man created God in his own likeness.

Among Christians, God is absolute perfection, while man is the repository of imperfections. Man, therefore, has to work and struggle all his life to reach a level of any attainable perfection while on earth to assume a divine relationship with God. On the other hand, among the ancient Greeks, their gods had to assume the imperfections of men to have any relation with them.

So Zeus, the head of the Olympian gods, was a perpetual womanizer of goddesses and mortal maidens as well. Hera was his ever-jealous and vindictive wife—and woe was she whom Zeus chose to have a love affair with. Aphrodite, the goddess of beauty and love, has the sexism that made her the idol of gods and men alike. And there was Hermes, the messenger god who carried Zeus' communication to the world below by flying and going from place to place, thus in charge of communication and transportation as well. And who would be more familiar to man than Mars, the god of war who keeps man and nations perpetually fighting and at war? No lesser than the gods was Hiphaestus, the artisan worker and laborer, the designer and inventor of the god's apparels and instruments for daily use in Olympus and elsewhere.

So in the likeness of man, the gods of an ancient religion kept themselves in constant touch with men in their daily affairs and activities—even taking sides as they did in the Trojan war.

But no matter what, from the ancient to the present, God is power—and man is always under that power. Man has only his prowess to pursue his destiny by rising above the confining limits of his humanity. This means rising superior above others with time, his image long forgotten and obliterated. Only his likeness remains—congealed in the memory he leaves behind.

This modern age is the era of image-makers who control the thinking of so many, especially in the field of politics, where a politician's victory depends on his good image. But, actually his image being promoted is not his looks and appearance, but his character.

Such character must emulate the best of those who had gone before him—the leaders and the heroes of the past, thus again is the confusion between image and likeness by the image-makers. Image is physical, whereby likeness is impression. One is appearance and personality; the other is impression.

And that is all there is to it. Both make the uniqueness of the total person.

# May the Better One Win

In my hometown where I grew up, there once lived two brothers whom the townspeople regarded as a sort of legend. Tommy and Jimmy were twins—identical twins who looked so alike that no one could tell one from the other. So usually, the question asked by anyone when the twins were not together was, "Are you Tommy?" or "Are you Jimmy?" The American slang, "the spitting image of the other," best describes the two.

Both Tommy and Jimmy were good-looking—tall, dark, and handsome—well-liked by everyone, especially the ladies. And well-groomed, too, having the same barber and tailor, who made them look more alike with the same crew-cut and clothes they wore. Their voice, too, sounded so alike that one had to peer closely to see who was talking. To make it easier the twins usually identified themselves first by saying, "I'm Tommy" or "I'm Jimmy." This happened when they were not together. And oftentimes, they were not—for they usually went their separate ways. Tommy was a homebody, while Jimmy was always out with friends having bachelor fun.

If both were so alike in looks, so were they opposite, as the north and south poles, so to speak, when it came to traits and character. Tommy loved staying at home, while Jimmy was a fun-loving, sociable person who always attended parties and social affairs. As students, Tommy was always with honors; Jimmy, on the other hand, almost always passed by the skin of his teeth. Tommy was always in the library, while Jimmy was in the gym practicing his basketball hobby, or in the cafeteria having coffee with the girls. They are so alike in their looks but are as opposite as night and day in their interests. However, Tommy and Jimmy were the best of friends, inseparable in the sense that nothing or nobody could come between them as brothers who loved each other.

Until, they fell in love with the same woman, a schoolmate. It was then that they became rivals, competing with each other to win the favor and love of Marlene, the woman they both loved. Tommy courted her with beautiful love letters; Jimmy wooed her with flowers and serenades, escorting her to dance parties, where he was at his best, since he was the best dancer in town.

But Marlene could not be won easily. For how could she be? She could not tell over one from the other. So she held them both at bay, which meant that she did not regard one more special than the other. She loved the intellectual Tommy, but she also loved and enjoyed the cheerful, fun-loving Jimmy.

But it could not always remain that way. She had to decide between the two. So choose she must. The townspeople, who were very much aware of what was going on, waited with bated breath for Marlene's decision. They took sides, even betting on who Marlene would choose. One even suggested that she toss a coin. In a small town during those old days, such a private issue was the town's affair.

Thus, Tommy's love letters became more ardent and fiery; Jimmy's serenades and love songs became more pleading. The courtship of Tommy and Jimmy for the hand of Marlene in marriage drew the wedge between the two. They no longer were seen together, for they went their separate ways. The twins were no longer even brothers who loved each other, the way they used to. It became a dilemma, for each one did not want to lose. To both, it was a do-or-die affair—a fight to the finish to win the woman they both loved. How alike they were in such a grim determination!

And so it was that it finally ended up with a fight between the two. It was a common occurrence during those years that two suitors for the same woman would fight each other by boxing. So in a duel Tommy and Jimmy, the inseparable twins, decided to fight each other until one dropped to the ground.

It was like the Superbowl for the townspeople as the date for the fight in the plaza, or public square, was approaching—everyone taking sides and even betting.

Only one person was not happy. Marlene was always crying secretly over what was happening—blaming herself for being the cause of it all. A few days before the big event, she went unseen to the twin's house to confront them. "Can you not give up this foolish thing you are doing?" she asked them directly as soon as the two let her in. There was anger in her soft voice. Tommy and Jimmy did not say a word, not knowing how to answer her, fearful that they might hurt her feelings.

So Marlene continued, "You, two, are not fighting for me. You are doing it for those people who are all having fun at your expense—and mine, too. I don't want to be the cause of you hurting each other, with hate in your hearts. For isn't that what is now happening? Hate. I came here to ask you to stop your fight. I refuse, and I will not be the prize for such fight."

Then Tommy spoke, "Only on one condition. Choose between the two of us—right here and now."

Marlene looked at Tommy, then at Jimmy, trying to make an instant decision. Then sadly, she shook her head and said, "I cannot do that now."

"So be it then," Tommy replied. "There is no other way. Fight we must, my brother and I. And may the better one win."

"Yes," Jimmy countered. "May the better one win."

Dismayed, Marlene shook her head and left. Surprisingly, Tommy and Jimmy shook hands. "May the better one win," they both said.

The day for the fight between the twins never came. For two days before the scheduled special event of the town came the sad news for Tommy and Jimmy. Marlene eloped with another suitor from a neighboring town.

In defeat, as in love, the twins showed their likeness more than ever before. They lost the woman they both loved. But in being broken-hearted, they emerged most alike.

Tommy and Jimmy never loved another woman again. They remained bachelors together—all their lives.

# 2

# Ego and Pride

## Narrative: Pedestals in the Mind

# Ego and Pride

" Know thyself." Merely two words of Socrates, the great Greek philosopher, but they contain all there is to know about human nature as seen and discerned in one person—the truth about himself.

That truth lies hidden within himself—he himself knows not where. Yet, it is more powerful than any part or organ of the human body because it dictates his thoughts and actuations, which leads to the formation of his character.

No persons are alike because of each's individual character. Even so, a person hardly knows his true character—the way he looks like. He only has to look at the mirror to know that. But what does his interior self look like?

His character determines that, but unlike the mirror, it does not reflect the truth. It is because human nature has a tendency to connect what's not praiseworthy about him, and keeps it hidden. Where? In his ego.

Everyone has ego. It is a part of one's being, because it serves as the repository of one's love for himself. Love is beautiful if shared with someone or with others. But he should love himself first so he would know how to love others. It sounds so natural and easy, but it is not so. It often happens that a man's love for himself rises above and transcends his love for others. This results in self-love or ego.

A person's ego is manifested in the two aspects of his human nature. One is his altruistic nature, which reaches outward toward others to share with them whatever good he could afford to give. Opposite that is his narcissistic self, which draws from people their praises, flattery, and adulation. This is something his ego needs to feed on, so he can elevate himself to a self-created pedestal of superiority that looks down on others—and thinks they look up to him.

What he isn't aware of is that those others shun him. They are either bored or annoyed by his conceit, which is the external manifestation of his ego. Thus, the intimacy of friendship is what the conceited person cannot have. Not that he cares, but the truth is that he is a lonely person because no one seeks his company. The lonelier he gets, the prouder he becomes, as if his pride is a shield to his loneliness. Behind all this, his ego is the silent manipulator.

It merges with pride to function as one. As ego swells, pride puffs up. The result is the conceited person. However, he cannot altogether be regarded as an unlikeable person. Despite his ego, he might have some fine qualities in him. Nevertheless, if he gets accepted by others, it is done more out of tolerance than of wholeheartedness.

This only goes to show that ego cannot dim out totally a person's fine qualities. In fact, if toned down, it can reflect valuable assets it develops within a person that enable him to attain success and honor—even if that would make him rise above others. "All is fair in love and war," as the saying goes, when it comes to success and achievement—ego or no ego. Humanity recognizes and accepts that.

But what humanity doesn't accept is what it cannot recognize—which is man's knowledge of himself. That is why Socrates' teaching, "Know thyself," confounds and challenges man until now.

For him to meet that challenge, he must, first of all, extinguish self-conceit obstructing his clear view and appraisal of his interior motivating qualities—his belief together with his understanding of his unique nature. They work as a compatible pair summed up simply as—believe to understand; understand to believe.

For instance, a man believes he can climb a high mountain because he has the desire, energy, and capacity to do it. But if he decides not to do it after all, it must be because of his fear that he might not be able to make it—either fall or die in the attempt. His belief comes first, and understanding of himself follows—the desire to, and the fear to do it.

It all sounds simple if that is all it requires to know oneself. It's not so. Something else lurks beneath one's belief and understanding of himself. That is his self-estimation of his true worth held in the gripping tentacles of his ego. If he succeeds in climbing the mountain, his worth expands his ego. In the process, he brushes aside the obtruding reality of his unworthiness if he succumbs to his fear. If he fails to climb the mountain because of such fear—then what? His ego won't permit that. It won't allow anything to lessen it, nor to hamper its growth.

So enters pride—which is ego's mate. By itself, pride stands supreme among man's various feelings because it exalts and gratifies itself in the good done by a person for the interests, welfare, and advancement of others. Whereas, the other side of pride dwells on the good done only for one's self—and is, therefore, called self-pride. This is what one uses to estimate his worth, which his ego exaggerates. No matter what, exaggeration in any form is not honest.

Paradoxically, however, honesty, which always speaks of true proportions and exactness, raises man's unworthiness far above the contrived height of his exaggerated worth.

If a person who believes he can climb a mountain, does it and succeeds in reaching the top, he gets the praises and adulation of all. Whereas, if he decides not to climb the mountain for fear that he might lose a footing and fall, which might even cost him his life, he is a failure, not only in the eyes of all, but to himself as well. Fear of risks and dangers accompanies every attempt taken to reach the top of the mountain, which symbolically means man's highest goals. Praises await him there.

Praise above life? How can all the adulation of the world compare with the value of one's life? Can the worth of praise exceed the unworthiness of fear that preserves life?

Ego does not answer such questions because they demand honest answers. Hiding behind the veil of untruth, ego does not allow truth to encroach in its domain. Can it win? Aristotle, another Greek philosopher, said, "The human mind seeks truth." What does this imply? Simply said, the mind is at war with ego. An untarnished mind seeking truth fights against its other side, which is sullied by ego.

But as a whole, the human mind has its defenses, when such a situation arises for it to face and settle. This often happens—the mind is endowed with intelligence and free will to choose the better side for the good of man.

By choosing the right side, which fights for truth, the mind becomes an impregnable citadel against its two powerful enemies that shelter and protect man's untruths—his ego and pride. Humility is the mind's weapon and shield against untruths.

However, man's ego cannot be easily defeated and vanquished. If driven against the wall, weakened by its own relentless attacks against the ever-increasing defensive strength of humility, it brings out its secret weapon. False pride, ego's cunning mate comes out into the open to fight humility.

Cunning as it is, with its sly, diabolical machinations, it even goes as far as pretending to be humility's ally until it finds a loophole through which it can knock down the truths surrounding and protecting humility.

A good example of this is when humility praises man for his good character and fine qualities that gave him success and honor. Ego's false pride goes along with such praises, for they also serve as the fodder it feeds on.

But when humility claims that man's fine character and qualities are gifts and blessings from man's Creator, the false pride shows its true colors. It claims that man's success and achievements are of his own making, not given by anyone here and above. It claims all the praises of man for ego to bask on. To do this, it distorts truth without straying away from it.

For instance, it can cite a divine teaching to suit its needs— such as "God helps those who help themselves." It nods its head in agreement. Then its hidden claws emerge and distort the truth with impunity. Man, helping himself, has to depend on his own reliance and self-sufficiency to make good in whatever he is doing to attain success and recognition. In other words, to rely on oneself leads to self-sufficiency; which recognizes no one for his high stature resulting from his personal achievements and successes.

Thereby, self-sufficiency is a good name for inflated ego as manifested in the pride of a conceited person. It covers up its bad side that makes it the enemy of humility, which teaches that all things a man needs in life—such as the food he eats, the air he breathes, and the water he drinks—come from his Creator. The best of all such gifts is love, without which life is empty.

Not that the egoist doesn't believe this, but that, with his air of self-sufficiency, he turns his back on this humble teaching—with a smirk.

Thus, a person's ego and pride block his reaching within the deep recesses of his mind where lies the truth about himself.

So it seems that Socrates' wise words to man, "Know thyself," would remain unanswered—now and forever.

# Pedestals in the Mind

I knew Martha way back in the past when we were teaching in the same school in Manila. I remember her quite well until now, for she was just a remarkable woman.

I consider her an intellectual, being a holder of a Master's degree, and was on her way then for her doctorate degree, besides being an honor student during her years in school. Besides that, Martha was admired more not only for her beauty, but for her loving nature toward her friends like me.

But so loving was she, especially toward one very special person—Jack, her husband. What was beautiful about it was that Jack loved her too—very much, until he decided to leave her.

Why? How could that happen to Martha and Jack, whom everyone considered as the paragon of marital bliss? I never realized until then that love could be devastatingly destructive until I saw it wreak havoc on two persons who loved each other, like Martha and Jack.

I remember that there was not a single day that Martha did not mention something about Jack—such as, "Jack did this," or "Jack said this," or "Jack gave this to me." It was so annoying sometimes that we just avoided listening to her.

But the crux of the matter was that she was telling the truth—and not boasting nor exaggerating. She was not playing it up. Jack really loved her that much. He expressed this in various ways by dating her out to dinner and movies, or going to night-clubs to dance like lovers.

Such love showed most especially in their home. What catches one's attention instantly upon entering their living room was the evidence of such love. The walls were full of pictures showing their loving togetherness from their wedding pictures and snapshots of them on various occasions. Virtually, the walls serve as an album for visitors to see and be impressed by the domestic bliss of such a home.

Even after Jack left Martha, those pictures remained on the walls. But she added something else. She hung all her diplomas and other pertinent certificates of honor in whatever vacant spaces left on the walls. It was as if she was saying something to Jack, such as: "You cannot find anyone like me."

After Jack left her, gone were her incessant talks to us, always praising him. Also gone were the boxes of chocolates on her living-room table that she offered to us every time we visited her, always saying "Jack gave this to me. Have some." What I missed most, however, was the vase of fresh roses on top of her piano. At the bottom side of the vase, which no one could see, was a pasted tiny card that read, "To you my love—from me." I was the only one who saw that card.

All such exhibits of Jack's love for her would not have gone awry, had she not have gone overboard by exaggerating the boxes of chocolates, which became more expensive, and the vase of three fresh roses that became a bouquet.

It didn't take long for Jack to notice them so ostentatiously displayed in the living room. This time he raised an eyebrow, as though asking himself, "What's going on?" It so happened that Jack and I met the next day at the bus stop where I was waiting for my ride home. I thought I said something nice to him when I said simply, "I was with Martha in your home yesterday. Those are beautiful flowers you gave her. And those chocolates! They really taste so good." All I expected was a simple "thank you" from him. Instead, he just looked at me glumly before he answered me.

"You are my wife's closest friend, aren't you?"

That surprised me, and so I looked at him directly as I answered, "Why, yes. But why do you ask?"

"It's okay, then. So I can tell you something I wouldn't say to anyone." Then he burst out, "I never sent her those goddamned things." And he left abruptly.

What Jack said rattled me. What did he mean? If he didn't give those "goddamned things" to Martha, then who did? Could it be that she has a secret admirer who could afford such expensive gifts? If so, she wouldn't be displaying that way for everybody to see, especially her husband. Who gets the praises and envy for such gifts? No one—but Martha. It hit me like a ton of bricks—Martha was sending those gifts to herself!

But why? As I kept on thinking about it, the more uneasy and disturbed I became. I felt in my bones that a domestic storm was brewing that would break out anytime.

I was right. It hit smack down on the home of Martha and Jack. It didn't take long. We just learned that Jack left Martha— home and all. It shocked everyone—but not me. The abruptness of it all! But I saw it coming—in fact, expecting it to happen any day. Sure enough, it did.

Of course, it had to do with those flowers and boxes of chocolates, the "goddamned things" he never sent Martha. He told me that in confidence, so I considered it a secret for me to keep. But it kept me wondering, and somehow I wanted to get to the bottom of it all. There was more than meets the eye, so I surmised that it would be more than those gifts to break a marriage. But what? A month after their breakup, I met Jack again at the bus stop. We had a long talk. He poured out all his feelings to me—his anger, bitterness, frustrations, and his question to himself. "Was it all because I did not love her enough," he asked me.

"No," I replied. "I think it was because she loved you only too well."

Jack shook his head in consternation. He did not understand the full impact of those words of a woman about another woman—me, about Martha. So I said, "Maybe we'll understand it better if you tell me what happened between you and

Martha before you decided to leave her. Perhaps that will help me put the pieces together."

"I confronted her with the truth about those flowers and chocolates of hers. The truth, and nothing but the truth, and no sidestepping it."

"What happened? What did she say?"

"What she said infuriated me. She said it was a private personal matter. 'Let me just say the flowers and chocolates were mere decorations and ornaments in the living room to serve as a conversation piece with visitors,' she explained.

"'So you can tell them that I sent them to you—is that it?'

"'So what if I tell them that?' she retorted, then added, 'After all, if you really want to, you can afford to send me those gifts yourself.'

"That stung me. I got hold of the box of chocolates and threw them out of the window. Then I grabbed the vase of flowers and was about to toss it out the window when I saw a small card sticking at the bottom side of the vase. I took it off and read it.

"'Why, this note is mine!' I blurted.

"She smiled as she said, 'It's good you remember. It was the card that went with the three fresh roses you gave me several years ago.'

"'Okay, but what's the big idea of placing them with those goddamned flowers of yours?'

"Still with her soft smile, she said, 'For my friends to read—and to eat their heart out.'

"'You mean to make them envy you. Is that it?'

"Yes, why not?" She replied defiantly.

"That did it. It was at that moment when I lost my respect for her."

"So you left her," was all I said.

Jack turned away from me as if gathering his wits to be able to unburden his thoughts to me—and how to say it. When he finally faced me again, I saw signs of unshed tears. I remained silent until he spoke again.

"Cannot a man love his wife without her shouting it at the rooftops? Because that's what she did every time she showed off to her friends those flowers and chocolates of hers with my love-card."

"Maybe it was just that she is proud of you for being such a good and loving husband, and that is the only way she knows how to say it," I said, trying to defend Martha.

"Proud? She was proud of herself—and she used me to express her self-pride," Jack replied vehemently. "She used me. That's the naked truth, and I cannot forgive her for it."

I was taken aback by the force of his accusation. "Used you? What do you mean by that?"

"It's like this," Jack started to explain something so emotionally complex and complicated. "To use me for her pride, she put me up on a pedestal in her mind to praise and admire me to her friends. But the truth is that it was herself she was praising and admiring all along. It is that damn ego of hers."

His voice broke and I saw him wipe a tear. I remained silent and just waited for him to say more.

"I truly loved my wife," Jack finally said. "But I truly wished that she could have loved me back without putting me up on a pedestal to satisfy her ego."

"So you left her," I repeated.

"Yes, because when respect is gone, love dies," Jack said simply.

# 3

# Talent and Skill

## Narrative: Man's Crowning Glory

# Talent and Skill

There is a saying—"The pen is mightier than the sword." The pen is used by a person with the talent for writing; therefore, it is inborn. The sword needs the skill to handle it and is developed through the constant practice and training by the person who uses it. Such skill is acquired.

In size, pen and sword are so different as to be compared at all. The pen is such a tiny device that it could be inserted in a small pocket or handbag; whereas, the sword needs a special scabbard tied to a heavy belt around the waist to carry it around. When the need for it arises, it could be drawn out from its scabbard with ease.

Why then is the pen mightier than the sword? By its size and weight alone, it is downright preposterous to even think it can wield more power and dominance over the sword. But that is the simple truth of its mightiness, which has been proven throughout the history of mankind's struggles for survival in both war and peace. Why so?

To answer that question, it is best to bring both pen and sword into another level of comparison beyond their opposite and incompatible qualities of size, weight, and shape. This step is to examine the purpose of each in terms of the benefit it brings for the good of humanity. Might is proven by the purpose, conceived and fulfilled by man, intended for his uplifting— through either constructive and destructive ways and means.

In this light, the pen is mighty indeed—so is the sword. But the question is—which is mightier?

The word "might" denotes power and strength to either protect or destroy. One verbal stroke of the pen could do that—so could one slash of the sword. So both could protect and uphold—just as they could destroy and devastate.

However, the pen, tiny as it is, has an abstract power all its own that—positively and absolutely—makes it mightier. It has loftiness. It is true that it can wreak havoc by the venom of words, but it can also bring to the heights such beauty and perfection, even beyond the realms of man's imagination, such visions that only the soul could see and understand. This is what the sword, with its size and sharpness, cannot do or evoke. Loftiness is, therefore, the purpose that makes the pen mightier than the sword. The sword can kill—but the pen can create. And this is precisely why talent—to which the pen belongs—is associated with the creative arts, such as: painting and sculpture, singing and dancing. Skill, on the other hand, comes later as the person grows and learns to use the other parts of the body—chiefly, his hands, legs, and feet—to build and construct, or play any kind of game and sport. Skill is acquired because it is the result of constant training and practice.

Be that as it may, both talent and skill are inseparable. Each is a part of the other. Talent conceives what skill makes or builds. In other words, skill is the exterior, concrete expression of interior, abstract talent. Each is dependent on the other—and both require professional training to improve and make perfect their basic fine qualities.

That is why there are schools of Fine Arts in high institutions of learning as universities; just as there are vocational schools to train and harness the various skills of man. Both kinds of schools—Fine Arts and Vocational—produce experts and specialists in the various professions and occupations engaging all kinds of human activities that use the mind and hands of man.

Furthermore, talent without professional training is raw material. For instance, a person with a beautiful singing voice cannot rise above the basic quality of his singing without professional training—thus depriving himself of the high levels toward which the hidden capacities of his singing could reach. Singing, like other talents, is art—and is called "voice culture." Tenors and divas, such as opera stars, are its finest products. Likewise, famous painters and sculptors are the products of professional and creative training.

Skill is the by-product of talent. Talent conceives what skill builds. For instance, an architect draws the structural designs of an edifice—but it is the carpenter who hammers in the nails to put it up. Fish abound in the broad, deep seas. Talent thinks of fishing boats and vessels with sophisticated fishing instruments that the fisherman uses for deep-sea fishing. And what is the worth of the finest silk without the thread and sewing machine of a dressmaker to make it a beautiful garment to be worn? Also, why is a woman willing to spend so much just to make herself beautiful in the hands of beauticians in a beauty parlor? The question is—what is talent without skill?

I remember a short story from my high school literature class that best answers this question. Its title is "Our Lady's Juggler" by Anatole France. Briefly, it is about Barnaby, a simple, ignorant man who earns his bread by the skill of his hands as a juggler. People who pass by stop to watch him performing his feat of throwing balls and knives up in the air, then catching and tossing them up again and again in various positions—standing, sitting, or lying in the ground. Passersby enjoy watching him and dropped coins in his nearby basket— his earnings for the day.

Barnaby is a very simple man who has only two loves—his juggling and the Blessed Virgin Mary, whom he does not fail to visit in the chapel after his day's work. He has no family or relative. Who will take care of him in his old age when he can no longer juggle?

Fate and chance answered that question for him. On his way home from the chapel one day, a monk happens to walk beside him. They talk to each other along the way and Barnaby pours out his problem to him. The monk invites Barnaby to enter the monastery. Barnaby accepts and becomes a monk because of his love for the Blessed Virgin Mary.

But even inside the monastery, Barnaby is unhappy. His brother monks compose and sing hymns to honor the Blessed Virgin. Barnaby cannot even read a note, so what can he offer her? The only thing he is good at is juggling. So that is what he offers her.

Without the other monks' knowledge, Barnaby does that secretly. But he cannot hide it for long. They follow him one day and see him juggling in front of the Virgin Mary's statue at the altar inside the chapel as he juggles joyfully all his pins, knives, and balls. Shocked by what they are watching, and believing that it is a sacrilege, they are about to throw the juggler out of the chapel, but something happens to stop them. Before their very eyes, they see the Blessed Virgin Mary become alive. She steps down from her platform, then approaches Barnaby. Miracle of all miracles! The monks watch with unbelieving eyes as she wipes the sweat out of the juggler's brow with the hem of her blue cape.

Heaven becomes an instant reality at that very moment. Its mystery is revealed in the divine display of acceptance and gratitude for the simplest, unalloyed offering of an ignorant man's skill—done out of love. All the composed hymns and songs of the talented monks put together pale and fade into insignificance when placed in heaven's scale that weighs the worth and value of human offering born out of talent and skill.

What determines such worth and value? It's none other than the love that accompanies the purpose behind the talent or skill of the person using it. No human action is wasted if done for that purpose; no matter how simple and insignificant it is. A delicious dish prepared by a simple housewife to make her family happy during mealtime is just as important and valuable as a bridge across impassable land and water, designed and build by an engineer to make man's traveling safer and easier.

Man has endless needs, so he goes on continually inventing, constructing, and building; also constantly training and practicing, to be able to use his talent and skill to the utmost—not only for himself, but all of mankind. That is his life's work and purpose. Behind it all is his well-used talent or skill. . ..

. . . and throughout it all, eternity watches with open doors, beyond which lies the awaiting rework for work accomplished— and purpose fulfilled.

# Man's Crowning Glory

By nature, I always love to watch people—not at just how they look like, but at their expressions, gestures, and mannerisms. It is like reading an unwritten book about the mysterious variation of human personalities. No two persons are really alike. They have their individual difference when acting or reacting in any given situation. I can even read one's thought by his facial expression. This interest of mine to watch people eventually led me to become a playwright.

I never knew I had a playwright's talent until I accidentally discovered it. This happened when I was assigned to handle a Drama Workshop at the university where I was then teaching as an English professor. To study drama and understand all the parts and aspects of a play, I had to choose one by a famous playwright for my class to read and analyze. One of my students made a suggestion that the class eagerly approved. Why not a play written by me? Surely, I must have written some plays; otherwise, why handle a Drama Workshop at all? That was what my students thought.

What could I say? The truth was that I had not yet written my play for the theater. I had written articles, speeches, short essays, and stories—but not a play. But instead of telling them the truth, I told my students to give me three days to make copies of my play for each of them to read before we study it in the class.

What a thoughtless answer! But I could not back out and change it. Without realizing it, I had placed myself in a tight fix—a "do-or-die" situation that needed an immediate result. Three nights to write a long one-act play fit to be staged in a theater? I knocked my head. I must be nuts and crazy to even think that it could be done by anyone—even by an experienced playwright. But it was too late to take back my words and promise to my students. My word of honor and respect were at stake. So write I must.

I "burned the midnight oil," so to speak, to keep my words. First of all, whom was I going to choose as my characters? They should be persons whom I knew well, so it would not be hard for me to reveal their traits and true character. Who? Why not my in-laws? I even smiled and snickered at the thought. How well I knew them indeed!

The plot? What happening or situation could bring them all together for something dramatic to happen? A timely event gave me the perfect answer. Recently, all in my husband's family—brothers, sisters, with their respective spouses—had just come from a family reunion because their father had just died. After the funeral, I witnessed how each one of my in-laws acted and behaved when the family lawyer read the last will and testament of the deceased. It was a perfect dramatic situation. It needed just a few touches of renovation and refurbishing, so to speak, of characters and plot to make an ideal, dynamic one-act play. The playwright's talent in me—which I never knew I had—started working. I entitled my play, THE REUNION.

My students enjoyed the play—and why not? Their teacher was one of the characters in a true-to-life situation that she was narrating to them with all its hidden details. It was a successful Drama Workshop that I shoved aside as one of my pleasant experiences as a teacher. What I didn't know was something more dramatic was already happening in my life because of that play. In fact, a miracle was taking place.

Without my knowledge, one of my students submitted my play to the ongoing annual "Palanca Literary Contest"—our country's equivalent of America's Pulitzer Prize. Never in my life had I ever considered to enter that contest that had produced our country's best literary writers and authors. It was beyond my wildest dreams to ever join their ranks. Just one Palanca Award would do that. Also, it would be a big boost to my writer's credentials in our country.

I got all that in one sweep. THE REUNION won First Prize—my first play written hastily in three nights! It was an overnight success and honor for an unknown writer like me.

But what made me happier was the prize money that went with the award. Five thousand pesos! In those days, that was a big amount for a young widow like me raising four children with a teacher's meager salary.

So the next year, I wrote another play, IDIOT BOY—again about my in-laws—which I now entered in the contest myself. It won again! So I wrote and wrote again each following year—not just for the honor, but more importantly—for there is "gold in dem dar hills" as the American slang expression goes. I aimed for the bigger prize money for three-act-plays, which also won.

For six consecutive years, I continually won the Palanca Awards for playwrights, until I could no longer join in the contest. Why? It was because the most prestigious prize was given to me—the "Hall of Fame" Award for Palanca Prize winners. It was then not yet awarded to anyone.

All of that I would not have attained, had it not been for my student who, without my knowledge, had the audacity to submit my play in our country's highest, most prestigious "Palanca Literary Contest."

Talent is indeed "death to hide," as Shakespeare says. It shows itself advertently or inadvertently in a person who has it. Insignificantly sometimes is its impact if left alone without any attempt to improve it by formal or professional training. My parents once had a female servant in our household—a maid as we call her in the Philippines—common in Filipino homes. I remember her quite well until now because of her singing voice. She always sang while working, with a voice that sounded like hundreds of birds singing together in the distance, made sweeter by the cooling wind that carried it to the listening ear. And she was just casually singing all her life. If properly trained and improved, it would have brought her to a higher state in life by public appreciation and recognition.

Skill can also do that for the person who has it, and decides to improve it with constant practice. More importantly, it can also be a means of livelihood for farmers, fishermen, carpenters, athletes, and so on.

Talent can win the world's honor and riches. Skill can win something higher than that. Just like the "Lady's Juggler" who won heaven by the skill of his hands, by merely tossing and catching balls up in the air to offer something to the Blessed Virgin whom he loved.

In simple terms, either talent or skill can be a person's crowning glory in life—if done out of love and service to others—for the uplifting of mankind—and humanity.

# 4

# Award and Reward

## Narrative: That's my Grandma

AWARD

REWARD

# Award and Reward

T he acme of a person's life is his success. This is realized only if he reaches his life's goal against the odds, hardships and challenges obstructing his path.

Consider a man who had always dreamed of climbing and reaching the summit of a high steep mountain – a feat not yet done by anyone! To realize such a dream, it would take him years and years of training and practice about mountain-climbing. More importantly, he must have a strong determination and will, undimmed by frustrations in failed attempts and failures. It is a passion dominating all other thoughts – that mountain summit must be reached, no matter what the cost. Such passion keeps him going – vibrant and full of zest.

The mountain summit has become the symbolic embodiment of his goal in life. It means either success or failure. Worse, it could mean life or death. To miss a step while climbing, or make a wrong one, would result in falling to the ground and just be a sorry mess of broken bones or a lifeless body.

But dark thoughts about the perils of climbing a high mountain, with hardly a jutting rock to hold on to, should be pushed aside by one whose sole purpose and goal in life is to see himself standing on that summit. So he has to move relentlessly upward, for there is no such thing as stopping midway between the top and the bottom when one is painstakingly struggling to reach his goal. Just like one does not stop midstream while swimming across a wide river, or else be swept away from the shore by swift currents. Or just like a racetrack runner who does not stop to tie his shoelace while racing against his opponents to reach the finish line.

So the finish line of a runner, or the mountain summit for the climber are the epitome of success for one whose goal is reached and realized.

If and when the climber reaches the top of the mountain, what awaits him there? What are the proofs and evidences of his success? People show them in pompous display as banners waving, showers of confetti in the air, trumpets blaring and people clapping, and so on. They are all the signs of man's triumph.

That many? Yes – even much more. They compose the prize in its multiple forms. But they are congealed into one, to be packed up and contained in a small object which the successful man can hold in his hands – such as trophy, a silver cup, a gold medal, an expensive item like a new car, a million dollars, or the symbolic key to the city which is a great gift to honor any prize-winner. They all come under one word – PRIZE.

A prize may also be called an award or reward. If a person is awarded the first prize, it means that he is the best among several competitors. So there is a winner as well as losers. It is but human to want to be among winners – not losers. So life is a perpetual struggle to compete and win against opponents or enemies – and winner takes all. This gives credence to the saying – "To the victor belong the spoils."

To win such "spoils" is an innate dream and ambition of men, as well as nations. It means to beat and defeat others so as to rise superior above them. The ulterior and overpowering motive behind it all is to "call the shots", so to speak, in human affairs, enterprises, rules and observance of laws, even ideologies.

In essence, "spoils" is competition. It draws the line between winners and losers – classified as follows – the great and the lowly; the rich and the poor; the powerful and the weak; the leader and the follower; the hero and the villain; the beautiful and the ugly; the saint and the sinner ..... and so on. They are the human results of competition.

Mankind is perpetually geared to feverish activities because of competitions. Without them, the world will fall into a rut because people will lose their impetus and zest for living which are kept burning in their hearts. How? It is by the envisioned promise of the prize – the award and reward awaiting one with work well done, excelling those of others.

So it is an instinctive desire of man to rise above the others – to be better, if not the best. That is why in all areas of human affairs and activities, competition is sure to take place. This is seen and observed in the various sectors of society – in schools and institutions of learning, in the business world, in politics and government, in labor and industries, especially in centers of entertainment, sports and games, mass media, even in religion, with the hierarchy of heads and leaders chosen for their shining record of religious work and service to God on His church.

Competition is always the name of the game because to rise in rank or position means increased income to afford one's basic material needs for food, shelter and clothing; also, some luxuries and improved life style. They make up the necessary essentials of living that command respect, admiration and honor – even the envy of others.

Such are the prevailing promises that go with a person's reaching the goal of his life. But to be able to do that entails winning competitions usually by contests. Since time immemorial, contests have become – advertently or inadvertently – the focus of man's energy and interest to cultivate and sharpen his capacities and capabilities to rise superior, and be recognized as such by all. To win contests is the gateway to such recognition.

Actually, what is a contest? What or who gave man such a concept, with all its ramifications to compete and fight one another to prove one's superiority?

Greek mythology of ancient times gave humanity its first glimpse and ideas about contests. When Eris, the goddess of strife was left uninvited to an Olympic feast of gods, in her vin-dictive wrath, threw the golden "Apple of Discord" inside the festive hall where the party was going on. On the apple was inscribed, "For the fairest." Thereupon the three most powerful goddesses rushed to claim the apple – Hera, wife of Zeus the head and leader of the Olympian gods; Athena, goddess of craft, wisdom and prowess in war; Aphrodite, the goddess of love and beauty.

No god in Olympus wanted to be the judge of that contest for fear of incurring the wrath of the losers. But the three god-desses insisted for the contest to go on because each one wants the honor and title as the "fairest." That was how the first beauty contest originated.

But who will be the judge? Zeus, in his omniscience, knew the most honest and impartial mortal below – Paris, the young and handsome prince of Troy. To get his favor and vote, each goddess offered Paris a gift: Hera offered him power and wealth; Athena would give him wisdom and superiority, espe-cially prowess in the battlefield; Aphrodite promised him the love of the most beautiful woman on earth – Helen, wife of king Menelaus, brother of Agamemnon, the most powerful king in Greece.

Paris chose Aphrodite. The result of the beauty contest in Olympus, home of the gods, was the downfall and destruction of impregnable Troy. It was the vengeance of the two losers against Paris and Helen. The Greeks under the leadership of Agamemnon waged war against Troy. Homer's immortal epic, the ILIAD is all about that war.

The concept about contest in Greek mythology also included one important and significant item about competitions. It is the prize that accompanies the contest – such as those offered by the three goddesses. In the course of time, the prize turned into a do-or-die thing to be won and awarded to the contestant, which is his very life.

In the arena of ancient Rome, the gladiators fought for their lives not only against hungry lions and tigers; but against another. The prize was either life or death granted by the emperor often influenced by the cries of the bloodthirsty crowds of spectators. If a gladiator fell to the ground, he had to remain lying there while his opponent stood above him waiting for the signal for him to thrust his weapon and kill the helpless loser. The signal was the downward flick of a heartless emperor's ignominious thumb. Life was the prize awarded by the mere flick of a thumb.

The savagery and inhumanity involved in these early contests that meant life or death for the contestants was carried on and on throughout history down to our modern times. But the savagery was toned down by civilized and more human means. This is now seen in the boxing and wrestling matches for the championship title. People would pay even a high price for a ticket to such entertainment.

Contests have become the panacea for modern man's boredom in his daily work and labor. Person versus person, team versus team, nation versus nation – these are the participants in various contests in the world today, such as the Olympic Games, the Miss Universe or Miss World Beauty Contests, chess tournaments, golf opens, and so on.

The nature of awards may vary, but the prizes to be won remain the same; only more alluring and captivating in their extrinsic and intrinsic value. To win such a prize would make a contestant an overnight success, a hero or idol – even the envy of others with the same dreams and aspirations for such goal in life.

Success is measured by tangible awards. Material gains and visible objects of victory make up an award. But the reward that follows the award is more priceless and valuable. It is immeasurable. It is only felt in the heart of the winner. It is the intangible evidence of his success, such as instant fame, honor and adulation of the world for its champions and heroes.

In short, award is world-given; and could only last that long. Reward comes from above, to lodge in the heart and memory forever.

## That's my Grandma

I used to live with my daughter and her beautiful family – her husband and two children. Proud to say, they are my two intelligent and smart grandchildren. I know them quite well since their very early years of childhood. Now one is an engineering student, and the other will also graduate soon as an architect.

This I can say about relationship with children and with grandchildren. They are not quite the same. Children look up to their parents as vital parts of their lives through their years from childhood to adulthood. Not so with grandchildren. In my case, they have love in their hearts for me, but not the nearness of dependence that draws them close to their parents. Nor do they look up to me for the authority to govern their lives which they recognize only in their parents. All this is due to the wide gap of age between our generations.

In other words, I no longer talk the same language with them. To them, I am already out of touch with the present world with its modern ideas and values, especially its rapid change due to technology. Computers, laptops, and modern gadgets are parts of their daily life as food and water. Whereas, I am using my pen, instead of the keyboard to do my written works – no matter how long, sometimes the length of a book. They lovingly call me "old-fashion Grandma," but what they mean is that I belong to the past, like fossil, with my antiquated ways and obsolete thinking especially about the moral and spiritual standards about human behavior.

My grandchildren's regard for me is further magnified by the fact that I have already limited activities outside and inside the home. I stay indoors most of the time with no household chores or work to do. So I am always in my room doing all my things – like reading, writing, watching TV, doing little things as sewing and knitting. Nobody bothers me.

It is only during mealtime, especially at dinner, when all in the family gather together; and when conversation takes place. But even in such conversation, I find myself more as a listener to the young ones who dominate in the talks which usually result in discussions or arguments. It is during all these verbal exchanges when I truly marvel at their knowledge and ability to express it so forcibly and convincingly – so far more advanced than mine when I was their age.

I had known even then that to gain the respect and recognition, especially admiration of the modern youngsters today, like my grandchildren, is not easy. They love me – yes. I can see and feel that everytime they say, "Hi, Grandma. How are you today?" But what I had never seen was the light in their eyes that show respect and recognition for someone they could look up to with pride and admiration.

To kindle such a light is not easy. Even a lifetime of showing one's worth would not do it. Unlike a nugget of dirt-coated diamond which would shine with constant rubbing and polishing. In other words, one cannot just "rub it in", so to speak, to show his inner sparkle. It would just shine in its pure light by itself in its own good time.

That time happened to me so unexpectedly. My grandson came home from school one late afternoon with more than his usual "Hi, Grandma" greeting. He gave me a hug! Of course I was surprised, but I knew better than to spoil it by asking why the sudden display of affection.

At dinner time that evening, I got my answer. He told us about what happened to him in school that day. He and his classmate were talking and comparing notes about their term papers, and how they were progressing in their research. This was his story....

"My classmate told me that his term paper about the history of the "Palanca Literary Contest" would be perfect if he could only interview one resource person."

"Why? What is it about this resource person that you want to know?" my grandson asked him.

"Her record as a winner of the Palanca awards is unsurpassed until now. Imagine winning six consecutive times! To top it all, she was given the highest and most coveted award of them all."

"What?"

"The Hall of Fame award."

"Why, that's really something!" my grandson said. "Who is this person anyway?" he casually added.

"Her name is Herminia Sison!"

"Why, that's my Grandma!" my grandson blurted out.

The light of recognition and admiration shone in my grandson's eyes as he was telling his story. It came at last. It shone even brighter when he turned to me and said, "I'm proud of you Grandma."

That was my reward from above — beyond the worth of all my world-given awards. I cherish it in my heart, and in my memory — always.

# 5

# Result and Consequence

## Narrative: The Black Sheep

# Result and Consequence

Everything that a man does is followed by a corresponding result. This is sure as day follows night. Flick the light switch and the dark room becomes bright. The result is instant. Strike a matchstick against a rough surface, and it produces fire. Let the stick remain in your hand until it burns itself out, and you will have burnt fingers. The instant result turns into a consequence. In other words, both result and consequence are the outcome of a certain act of doing things.

Man's life is all about doing things, and letting something to happen and ensue. This is his instinctive anticipation—either conscious or subconscious—of the result or consequence of his act. Otherwise, life would be mere existence. In simple term, a man's life is governed by the result and consequence of his act on everything he does.

And all that he does—what are they for? For an animal, all that it does are for its basic needs and means to survive—and thereby exist. For man it is much, much more than that. Briefly, it is to attain a purpose to reach a goal—and, thereby, realize his ambitions and dreams. To be able to do that, he must have a direction to follow toward the summit he has to reach.

Profoundly, it is the direction that a man follows in his journey through life. Without such direction, he will just be going around in circles with no destination. A man has his own destination, which starts at the very moment he is born. Birth and death are the only true, immutable realities of life. It is between both that a man's direction starts and ends toward his destination. Where?

To think about that makes a man pause and ponder deeply. The grim finality of it all! No return trip. No chance at all to come back and live life all over again for better results and consequences. Where his destination ends is a place of no return, where all he has done on earth will be weighed and judged no longer by worldly values.

Be that as it may, man is given by his Creator the freedom of choice to determine his destination by the direction he chooses to follow in life. Simply, it is choosing between right and wrong. Symbolically, to go left is the wrong way; just as turning to the path at the right is the correct way. To choose wisely, a man is endowed with intelligence and fine instincts—no matter who or what he is—to make his choice.

For instance, if a student does not study well, he will have failing grades, and may not graduate at all. If one drinks a lot of wine, he becomes an alcoholic. If he eats too much sweets, he will have diabetes. If he smokes a lot, he does much damage to his lungs. If he gambles a lot, he will end up being bankrupt. And if he is selfish and greedy, no one will love him. Finally, if he has no faith and chooses not to believe in anyone beyond himself, he will not know how to hope.

Praying goes hand in hand with hoping—and together, they constitute the higher human act of all. They make him look at the past to foresee the future—thus enabling him to choose the path he has to follow. The essence of hoping and praying is to help one's self first—not just lying supinely on one's back, waiting for manna to fall from above. And it is in such acts of helping one's self that brings about good results and consequences.

In allowing one's self to wallow in wanton indulgence to idleness and worldly pleasure is to have a meaningless life that leads to a dim future and destination. The general and highest principle of life is always doing things for good results and consequences. That is why there are rules of life to follow.

Result and Consequence

Animals do not have such rules of life to follow. They just act—and that's it.

No, not for man. "Look before you leap," is the famous slogan that guides man before acting. Even in blind rage, he wouldn't just point a gun at someone and kill him on the spot. He knows only too well that it is breaking the rule of life contained in the Ten Commandments from above—"Thou shalt not kill." Dire consequences are sure to fall on a person who breaks even one of those Commandments. It is bringing down damnation upon himself.

This is the worst consequence of them all, unknown to man's worst imagination. The Biblical injunction of six short words could best explain it—"The wages of sin is death."

That means hell.

# The Black Sheep

This is a short account about a family I well knew way, way back in the past. It is a family of parents with seven children which was regarded very highly and respected in their community—and why not?

Though not rich, it was a good Christian family with hard-working parents and children with school honors . . . except one who went astray. He became the black sheep of the family.

The father was a geodetic engineer or surveyor. Though he worked hard all his life, he was not able to amass wealth; except for a small farm and fishpond. All his earnings went to the education of his children. There was no scrimping when it concerned the educational expenses of his children. The outcome of such parental devotedness and dedication was that all the children became professionals—an engineer, a doctor, two teachers, a nutritionist, a businessman—and one who was a failure. He didn't finish his college degree. He was about to enter the College of Medicine when he fell into a bad company of idlers and wine drinkers. It did not take long for his demise to surface. His failing grades resulted in his enrolling in the same subjects again. He dropped out of college and spent his time with his bad company.

The consequence of his wrong-doing was heavy on himself. His failure became a rut from which he was unable to extricate himself. He was a failure as a person, as a son, and as a husband. He married, but after a few years, his wife left him. Consequence could have a domino effect—one failure after another.

A church teaching says: "Narrow is the gate to heaven; wide is the path to perdition." When perdition takes its toll, downfall is the consequence. It is actually falling down—swift and sure. The ascent toward the summit is hard and arduous; the descent to the abyss is swift and deadly.

Thus it is that the black sheep of a good Christian family resulted in the unhappiness of all its members. The mother prayed "novena after novena," while the father spent more time on his knees in church. But it did not alleviate their sorrow over one black sheep among their children.

Indeed, wide is the path to perdition. The consequence is great on the black sheep, but it is heavier on the family. I saw that in the secret tears of the mother and the father—the unhappiness in their faces even when their successful children were around them.

I saw it all with sorrow in my own heart. Why? It is because I'm one of their seven children

# 6

# Happiness and Sadness

## Narrative: Don't Leave Me . . .

# Happiness and Sadness

There is a phrase man commonly uses to express a feeling wrapped up in his attitude—which is his "state of mind." This has to do with his two feelings—happiness and sadness. Between these two is the spectrum of all other feelings known to man. If life is compared to a tapestry of colors, happiness is the right side, and sadness is the other and wrong side.

Everyone, with no exception, wants to be happy. In fact, sadness is caused mainly by one's not being able to attain it, or lose his sources of it. Such sources are cropping up everywhere for man to find his happiness through pleasure, fun, and enjoyment. The world is full of such places ablaze with lights, of blaring music and loud sounds, the deafening noise of traffic and markets—all of them beckoning man to satisfy his various appetites for body, mind, and spirit according to his material human needs. Such sources are also alluring him to fill up his sensual desires for wine, women, and song. More than all of these desires is man's wilder spirit to go after the "unreachable stars" blinking at him from unknown distances.

So he goes off to foreign lands and places far away from his home. He transports himself through land, water, and air—such as guided tours, pleasure cruises, and long car, train, or bus trips—to get near the "unreachable stars" of his desires.

Man is born with such "stars" to reach out for. They are the symbols of the purposes of this life given to him from above.

To fulfill his purpose is to find his happiness. To fail is the cause of his sadness.

This applies to all—king and peasant alike. Some are born for a high and great purpose, and are, therefore, endowed with wealth and power to pursue and fulfill his purpose. The majority of mankind born in lowly state, such as workers and laborers, are equipped mainly with the bare essentials for their needs to keep them alive and to survive the world's onslaught against their poor state.

But happiness is not to be claimed by either the mighty or the lowly. It doesn't choose on whose side it should be. Rather, it sets its own level for either to reach—which is found in his "state of mind." It is where it lies—shining from within a person's being—or casting a shadow or gloom over his features and expression.

I remember a short poem that best illustrates both happiness and sadness in two persons. I remember it quite well because I was made to read it in front the class when I was a first-year high school student way back in 1936. The title of the poem is "The Miller of Dee" by Charles Mackay. It is about a king asking a lowly miller working by the river Dee a question that concerns them both. Quote:

And tell me now, what makes thee sing,
With voice so loud and free,
While I am sad, though I am king,
Beside the river Dee?

The king's sadness must have been great and heavy, for he said to the miller. Quote:

For could my heart be light as thine,
I'd gladly change with thee.

The miller doffed his cap to the king in humility and obeisance as he sang his answer; quote:

"I earn my bread," quoth he;
"I love my wife, I love my friend,
"I love my children three;
I owe no penny I cannot pay,
I thank the river Dee,
That turns the mill that grinds the corn
That feeds my babes and me."

In these lines of the miller is found the primordial sources of man's happiness, which are—love of family and neighbor; his gratitude to Nature that provides the sources of his work to earn for his basic needs for food, shelter and clothing; more importantly, giving him contentment with what he has, no matter how humble. For it is discontent that gives rise to envy of others. It is envy that brings out one's selfishness, greed, and avarice—the very instrument of hate against happiness in man.

Our teacher then did not teach us the valuable lessons found in that short poem about the miller and the king. Either he did not understand the depth and wisdom conveyed in the seeming simplicity of the poem beyond its beautiful rhyme and rhythm; or, if he had that wisdom at all, how could students in their very young teens be mature enough to understand such lessons about life?

It has taken me a lifetime to learn the poem's valuable message, which I am still learning until now. The path that one must travel through all his life is strewn with woes and travails that he has to undergo to realize that living is simply made up of both happiness and sadness inextricably side by side together. They represent all of life's other opposites, such as—night and day, light and darkness, right and left, beauty and ugliness, sweet and sour, far and near, up and down, tall and short, and so on and on. Most especially among all of such opposites are the absolute natural opposites of life and death—and, finally, the highest supernatural opposites of heaven above and hell below.

All of life's opposites confronting man every moment of his life prove only one thing—that he has the innate right to choose. His destiny rests upon such choice. Basically, the choice is between happiness and sadness. And it happens right within him—in his own conscience.

Man's conscience is his and his alone—and no one knows what's in it, except his Creator. However, what's in one's conscience manifests itself in many ways. One is when he wakes up in the morning with an unbidden song in his heart. This means that he had a good night's sleep undisturbed by cares and problems; and he is looking ahead to the new day's promise of pleasant work and activities. On the other hand, somehow he is tired and unrefreshed from having been tossed about in bed all night because of a nagging sense of guilt in his conscience over something either done or not done—no matter how trivial—that works against the good and welfare of others.

However, it is in sadness where man is more meditative and contemplative—even creative. It is the tone of sadness that Wordsworth heard in his long poem—"Tintern Abbey," which he describes as "the still, sad music of humanity." Or what John Keats said in his poem "Ode to a nightingale": "The sweetest songs are those that are fraught with saddest thought."

And much more eloquent is how Matthew Arnold bewailed the sadness of humanity in his poem "Dover Beach." Quote:

Ah, love, let us be true
To one another! For the world, which seems
To lie before us like a land of dreams,
So various, so beautiful, so new,
Hath really neither joy, nor love, nor light,
Nor certitude, nor peace, nor help for pain . .

These lines in Arnold's poem give us the key to open the door to happiness. The key is love. But it is a key that is found only in the ointment of sadness, which paradoxically produces the brightness and glow of happiness filtered through the combined mind, heart, and soul of man.

72

# Don't Leave Me . . .

D on Manuel lived in a big, sprawling bungalow in the out-
skirts of Manila way back in the past, before World War
II when the Japanese forces attacked and destroyed the city.
Along with such destruction was Don Manuel's beautiful resi-
dential property.

One's wealth and prominence, even in such a small country
as the Philippines, was displayed, even until now—in the resi-
dential opulence seen in the size of the area where the family
house was built. That determines if it could be called a "villa."

Don Manuel's place was called "Villa Paz" in honor of his rich,
old wife—Tia Paz, as we in the family called her. I remember the
place quite well, because my family used to be invited there for
special occasions. I was quite awed by the whole place. It was
really a big, wide area for a house and its surrounding yard. If
one had to walk in a fast pace from the main gate, it would take
him more than five minutes to reach the house's front door. The
whole area of Villa Paz was a hectare, full of fruit-bearing trees
and various plants, even some coconut trees. Behind the sev-
en-bedroom bungalow was the servants' quarters—a duplex
house, the larger one occupied by Tomas, the life-long chauffeur of Tia Paz. He lived there with his wife, Ana, the villa's
housekeeper.

Although Tia Paz was fifteen years older than her husband,
Don Manuel, they loved each other and were quite content with
their life together, except for one thing: they were childless.

They were not happy despite their busy social life. They had no heir to inherit their wealth and property—especially Villa Paz.

So they thought of adopting a child and raising it as their own. It had to be a newborn baby. It happened that Don Manuel's poor brother had the answer. He already had five children, and his wife was about to give birth to another one. Don Manuel and Tia Paz took the baby girl as soon as she was born and named her Cita. They never bothered about legal adoption papers, for Cita's parents gave her to them willingly and gladly. They already had many children to raise and feed. Besides, Cita would be the heiress of a very rich couple—their own close relatives.

But unpredictable Fate could bring unthinkable situations to test man's best intentions and desires. Everything in Villa Paz was fine with everyone happy over Cita, who had brought such delight and brightness to the household. Then something happened. Ana, the wife of the chauffer, Tomas, was going to have a baby. And just at the very same time, Tia Paz conceived and was going to have a baby at her rather late age!

What joy it was for Don Manuel, and especially Tia Paz! Now they were going to have their own child to be the heir to all their wealth and fortune. Poor Cita was shoved in the background amidst all their joy and excitement.

They were born almost at the same time of the month: Gloria, the rich couple's daughter, and Carmen, the baby girl of Tomas and Ana. And so it was that they both grew up together in Villa Paz, as playmates and friends, together with Cita, who was only a few years older than they. Villa Paz became a brighter, happier household with the sounds of children playing and laughing all over the place—until insidious thoughts about material wealth and possessions crept into the minds of Tia Paz and Don Manuel. Why share their daughter's inheritance with another one, Cita, who was not even a legally adopted daughter? It did not take them long to decide. They agreed to give Cita back to her parents.

This they did with no qualms of conscience or sense of guilt or remorse about Cita's welfare, who was not their daughter. It was an emotional jolt to a young, innocent child.

But again, Fate had something up its sleeves, so to speak, to test man's conscience and intentions while seeking his happiness and peace of mind. Somehow, and in some inscrutable ways, Don Manuel and Tia Paz had to pay the consequence for commiting such a cruel act—a crime without a name—which cut and demolished the tie and bond of love and friendship between persons. For what? For selfishness and greed over money and riches and, most especially for Don Manuel and Tia Paz, the proud name of Villa Paz, which was the symbol of their wealth, prominence, and aristocracy.

The consequence came too sudden and quickly. Gloria, their daughter and heir, got sick and died.

The sorrow and sadness of the rich couple knew no bounds. Since then, they spent less time in Villa Paz. They kept on traveling abroad, going to various places in the world, to escape from what was gnawing their minds and hearts. But they could not get away from themselves. For how could they escape from the sadness within themselves?

It was worse for Tia Paz. She lost all zest for life, and she just wasted away in her inconsolable grief, which neither time nor the world's pleasures could heal. It did not take long. She died of pneumonia caused by a bad cold she caught by staying long in the open air beside her daughter's grave.

Don Manuel was left to live alone in Villa Paz—now empty and desolate. What was there to live for without his wife and daughter? Even his poor brother, who sometimes brought Cita to visit their sorrowing rich relative, failed to diminish his sadness—although Cita was the only one left who grew up close to him. Perhaps he would think of taking her back to Villa Paz again. This he did, but his brother—out of hurt and pride—refused to give Cita back to him. After what he had done to Cita so despicably? Throwing her back to her poor parents when he had a child of his own? Not wanting anyone to share in their daughter's inheritance—not even Cita, whom they adopted when they were childless? So let him rot in his riches!

But again Fate stepped in with something up its sleeves to test the fine nature of man being molded by the chastening effects of sadness. Carmen, the daughter of his chauffer, Tomas and his wife, Ana, became his source of consolation. He watched her grew from childhood to a charming, intelligent lovable person. He always saw his daughter Gloria in Carmen.

Young Carmen was always by his side, either inside his home or strolling along its wide yards—delighting him with her endless girlish talk and chatter. She virtually nursed Don Manuel back to his former self—not only physically, but emotionally as well. Carmen filled up the emptiness in his heart.

Time passed by. Carmen studied nursing. As soon as she graduated, she applied for a nursing job in the United States, where hospitals were always in demand for good nurses with the assurance of a high salary and a bright future. Carmen's plan to migrate included her parents—Tomas and Ana. She would petition for them as soon as she could get herself settled in the States.

Don Manuel knew all of Carmen's plans. How he hated her plans! But what could he do? She had her own life to lead, and he had no right to hinder or obstruct her from pursuing her best interests for herself and her parents. No matter what, he dreaded the day Carmen would leave him. She was the only consolation he needed in his remaining years. She was the last link to whatever happiness could be squeezed out of the years ahead. Was she not born at the same time as his daughter, Gloria? Carmen was his daughter by his love and affection for her that he was never able to give to Gloria. That thought made him much sadder.

Meanwhile, Carmen continued to nurse him—this time, professionally. How he loved every moment of her tender care! How could he go on living without her? But someone had to take her place—a professional nurse like her. They found one in the hospital where Don Manuel used to go for treatment and cure of his illness.

The day came for Carmen to leave. It was on that day that Don Manuel cried unashamedly as he said to Carmen, "Don't leave me." She embraced him lovingly, and with tears also in her eyes, she told him, "I'll come to visit you when I have a long vacation from work."

That vacation from work took a much longer time to wait for. Before it could happen, Fate dealt its final blow. The nurse hired by Don Manuel to take care of him turned out to be a scheming fortune hunter!

Cunningly and slyly, she used her position to steal the wealth and material possessions of Don Manuel—including Villa Paz. First of all, she enamored herself to the affection of her ailing patient until he was convinced that the only way he could keep her permanently was to marry her.

What followed was the inevitable tragic end of Don Manuel, who paid the consequence of violating one's conscience to choose between right or wrong—which means either happiness or sadness.

The nurse who was a heartless, unscrupulous fortune hunter succeeded in her devilish schemes. What poetic justice! For was not Don Manuel himself a fortune hunter when he married Tia Paz with all her riches and property—especially Villa Paz?

Perhaps Don Manuel realized, to his dismay, that happiness could not be found in pompous surroundings and luxuriant living. That was what caused him to cry out to Carmen, "Don't leave me."

Was it a cry about his losing his only source of happiness with Carmen leaving him?

Or was it a cry of utter sadness; or of enveloping despair?

# 7

# Desire and Passion

## Narrative: Life's Sweetest Gift

# Desire and Passion

Love at first sight is an expression among romantics. It is beautiful, but there is something not right about it. How can a person love someone he doesn't know? And at first sight at that? It takes so much, much more for love to develop. It just doesn't happen in an instant, just like attraction.

For instance, a male is easily attracted by a woman's beautiful face, her shapely body and legs, her eyes, her lovely tresses, and other physical attributes. That attraction ignites another feeling in the beholder—which is wanting what he sees. This is aptly called desire. Should not the romantic expression be "Desire at first sight" instead? Love can happen later, which depends on what it is fed on and kindled—no other than the flame of passion. In other words, desire and passion are the two ingredients of love, without which it cannot be aroused and kept alive and burning.

Is there any person without love in his life? None. At least he has the love of a mother, a brother, or a friend. No one is exempt from love, because it is the reason and purpose of his existence. Man is born to love and be loved. Desire and passion keep a man's love alive throughout his life.

The crux of the matter is that man cannot love alone. It takes two to love—the one who loves, and the other who is loved. Such a feeling between two persons is the most profound mystery of creation that has never been unraveled, or dissected as in a microscope to know its components, or what substance it is made of, to make us understand why it is God's greatest gift to man, his best and highest creation.

To have a broad and clear idea about what the mystery of love is, it is best to go to the root and origin of it—desire and passion. What is desire? To put it simply, it is an urge to have, hold, and possess what one wants. For instance, a woman who is shopping sees a diamond ring displayed at a jewelry shop that attracts her attention and interest. Desire at first sight takes place. The longer she looks at it, the more she wants it. So buy it, she must.

How? The object of her desire is expensive, beyond her means to afford it. She has to find ways and means to raise the amount needed to buy it—no matter what.

So with all the ardor of her heart, she drives herself relent-lessly, surging on to find means by which she could have and possess the object of her desire—to see the diamond ring sparkling around her finger. That ardor of her heart is the flame of passion.

Because of the urge of desire, the inflamed mind and body combine to produce the white heat of passion to surge on toward the acquisition of the thing one wants so much. Thus, it could be said that the summit and acme of one's life is reached by passion that started from desire. For between the two are all the dreams, visions, ambitions, and goals of man—the entirety and sum total of his life and the memories and legacy he leaves behind after death.

Due to the idea about desire and passion, the greatest love stories have enriched history, from ancient to modern time. The beginning and origin of love is known to have sprung up from mythology—the earliest possible time that man's thinking could reach, to relate himself to the actual unchanging reality and essence of life, which is love.

Who could be more immortal in the mind of humanity than Helen of Troy? The most beautiful woman of ancient Greece, who left her husband, king of Mycenae, to elope with a total stranger—Paris, prince of Troy, who was shipwrecked and washed ashore in her land. When Paris opened his eyes he beheld Helen, who was then strolling along the beach. Desire for such unbelievable beauty at first sight sparked within Paris, igniting instant passion—and as they talked, love was shortly to follow.

This love they both accepted without question or doubt as to what destiny had demanded of them—which was to be together all their lives, at any cost or price. Because of this, a mighty kingdom had to fall. Troy's impregnable walls fell under the mightiest and unseen force of all—love. The desire and passion at first sight between Helen and Paris burst into love that no human power could conquer or vanquish—especially because it was forbidden love.

So they eloped. This caused all of Greece's separate state-kingdom to unite to war against Troy when Helen lived in bliss in the arms of her prince lover. The Trojan War lasted ten years—but the memory of Helen of Troy has lasted through the centuries to the present.

Thus, mythology started humanity's great love stories ignited by desire and passion. What would lovers give up for it? Cleopatra, the queen of Egypt, the mighty empire in the ancient past, gave us the answer. She surrendered her kingdom to Rome and ended her life by the bite of an asp, the deadliest snake—all for what? For love of Anthony, who had been sent by Rome to conquer her land. What happened? They were smitten by desire and passion for each other, then engulfed in the fiery embrace of consuming love.

Cleopatra and Anthony were lovers in the remote past. What do our modern times have to show as their counter-part, who because of smoldering desire and passion, a mighty kingdom had to be surrendered and given up?

The twentieth century has given us one such counterpart to those ancient lovers. King Edward VIII, bachelor uncle of England's present queen, Elizabeth II, gave up his throne—one of the few mighty nations of modern history—for what? For passionate love that neither power nor riches could subdue—which was his love for an American divorcee, Mrs. Wallis Simpson. The world gasped in shock. So what? To the dethroned king, what would life be without the woman of his desire, passion, and love by his side?

No less did the world gasp again when Prince Charles of Wales, son and heir of Elizabeth II, separated from the most beautiful and the world's beloved Princess Diana, who, to top it all, already bore two sons, future successors to England's throne.

This time, the world looked away—not able to understand why Prince Charles, heir to the England's throne, had to separate from his very lovely, beautiful, and the people's most beloved wife, Princess Diana. For whom? For someone not yet known nor accepted by the people to replace Princess Diana. The rest is history. But to look at it closely, it is the story of desire and passion that make even kingdoms shake in their very foundations.

"The world loves a lover," as the saying goes; but that depends on the beauty, truth, and honor behind such love that seek to reach upward for its fulfillment—not to sink into the mire of worldly lowliness.

In other words, the summit and peak of one's life is passion spent in quest for something that started from desire. For between the two are all the dreams, visions, ambitions, and sum total of his life and death together.

For isn't that what the stories of the greatest passions of men in history are all about? Christ gave His life for love of man. That was His passion—without which there would not be Redemption. From it, we learned that love is sacrifice—sacrifice even of life itself.

Who can be better characters to illustrate this than Shakespeare's Romeo and Juliet? They became the world's symbol and byword for immortal lovers—because they defied everything that stood between them, such as family, friends, institutions, even the world, if need be. They could not live together, but no one was able to stop them from dying together.

Two other literary characters, Evangeline and Gabriel, who were forcefully separated on their wedding day, became immortal lovers because they spent their whole lives searching for each other. The passion spent to find each other is the theme of their love tragedy. They did find each other at last, only when Gabriel was dying. They were reunited at the last moment before Gabriel died in the arms of Evangeline.

Almost all of the world's immortal love stories have a common ending—which is two lovers choosing to die together, rather than live without each other. So, what is this most powerful force that man, with all his strength, intellect, and ingenuity, had to contend with, yet always overpowered by it? Man may conquer nations, but love can overpower him. That is why love is perennially a mystery. Man will never understand it, nor will he ever be able to define it.

Elizabeth Barret Browning came nearest to defining it by expressing her very own feeling of love for her husband, Robert Browning, in her poem, "How Do I Love Thee?" The last lines of that poem gives us, at least, a clue to what this mystery of love is all about. Quote:

I love you with the length,
breath, depth, and height
my soul can reach;
and if God chooses,
I shall but love thee better
after death.

Man's existence could perhaps be seen in its totality by putting together in a capsule his desire and passions. Desire impels, while passion compels him to surge forward to discover the reason for his existence. That capsule could fittingly be labeled LOVE.

Therein lies the mystery of love—desire and passion that enable man to rise from the confining limits of his imperfection to the unreachable heights of perfection. This is made possible by love alone. No matter what, love still remains a mystery. Why?

Because love is infinity—boundless, beyond the reaches of man's thoughts, unfathomable to any human being, even when he loves. Only his desire and passion can give him a glimmer of it.

And that's all that man needs—just a glimmer of what love is that would make him understand why he is human.

Why is it human to want more millions after amassing his first million dollars? Why is it human to want more than he can grasp? After becoming a governor, he wants to be his country's president. After traveling in Asia, he wants to go to Europe and all around the world. Being an employee, he wants to be boss. In other words, there is no limit to man's desire. More so, there is no end to his passion to realize and possess what he wants.

Could it then be said that love is merely the by-product of desire and passion. Can it not emerge in one's heart by itself?

Perhaps the answer is with us all along—each one of us. Because we were born with it, to live with it—on toward eternity where we came from—and where we are going ultimately, at the end of the day.

# Life's Sweetest Gift

The largest private university in the Philippines, and most possibly in Asia, started from a two-classroom of around thirty students. Within a few years, its enrolment had skyrocketed to more than fifty thousand students—each year rising to several thousands more coming from all parts of the country. Phenomenal, to say the least.

Who was behind it all? Who was the planner, builder, and architect of this educational institution? A genius? No. He was a teacher all his life, who rose to be the dean of the College of Business Administration of a then city's famous private university. All through the years of his teaching career, he toyed with the idea of having a school of his own—and why not a college if at all? From a mere idea arose a desire, so strong that he dared himself to turn such desire to reality. What did he need to do? A few years before retirement from his job, he resigned. At the age of fifty-seven, he went to work to create a school of his own. He rented two rooms of a building located in the city's busiest section and started the nucleus of his school—review classes of students who were preparing for the yearly board examination for Business Administration graduates. With him were two colleagues of his who were willing to go along with his ambitious plans. The three of them handled the review subjects in the two classrooms of thirty students. That year's topnotcher in the B.A. board exams came from those two classrooms. And, so with the following years.

By now, from the ashes of World War II that ravaged the city of Manila, arose, as the proverbial Phoenix, the nation's largest university. The post-war era was characterized by the flood of students whose higher education was arrested by the four years of Japanese occupation.

It was the perfect time for the founder's desire to become a reality. And what a result it was—beyond all his wildest dreams! Like mushrooms, one building after another arose overnight—until that busy section of the city became the campus of several colleges offering all professions to education-hungry students. The golden years of this university took place when its founder was its president and chairman of the board, with his two colleagues holding important positions.

During those years, I was a faculty member as English professor. A university magazine was then to be launched, whose main feature was about the founder. I submitted an article about him—and it made a hit. I was told to go to the president's office. At last I was face-to-face with someone I had read so much about, who then had become famous. We talked about my article. He might had been pleased by my responses to his comments, and answers to his questions because, thereupon, he took a page from some papers on his table and told me to read it in front of him. Then he asked me, "What do you think about it?"

"What's it all about," I questioned him.

"They're the opening paragraph of a book about the history of our university. Just give me your opinion or your thoughts as a writer about these opening paragraphs."

"Okay, then," I answered with much ado, "I think they're well written. But they are just beautiful words. That's why I asked you what they're all about."

He sighed a little and said, "You´ve told me enough. I got my answer and I agree with you."

Peremptorily, he took the rest of the pages on his table and threw them into his waste box. "There . . . that settles it," he said.

"Settle what?"

He paused awhile, as if thinking deeply, then replied, "You see, I asked a well-known writer—in fact, commissioned him to write my book, the book of my dreams and desire—the history of my university. I already gave him a down payment for such commission, but I'll consider that as down-the-drain payment. I am giving you the commission to write my book instead of him. He's done!" He then disclosed the name of that writer—who was well-known among the country's writers, especially among journalists as being a famous columnist.

So I said, "Sir, you are going to change a famous writer for an unknown one like me? His name alone as author of your book will attract many readers. Think again."

"I don't have to. I know what I want. I prefer your style of writing."

Before I could answer, he hastened to add, "More important to me is the depth of your ideas. It's as if you read what's in my heart. I think they call that insight. That's a gift, but not all writers have that."

"Thank you, sir."

"Now tell me, what's your approach in writing my book?"

"First of all, if I accept your offer, I must have at least a month or two to do some research, and to find out if I can handle the writing of such an important book, which to me will be part of your legacy as founder of your university."

He beamed as I shared my thoughts with him.

"I like what you are saying. Go on, say some more," he urged me.

So unabashedly, I went on, "As to my approach in writing it, history is only a part of a biography—your biography. In other words, the book will be about the history of the university as the major part of the founder's biography."

"Do you need money for your research?" he asked, as if I had already agreed to write his book.

To which I simply replied, "I'll let you know when and if I find myself capable and ready to write it."

He then placed both his hands on my shoulders, a gesture that seemed to say that the contract about his book was already sealed. Then he said with a solemn note I detected, "As to my biography, my life is now an open book to you. Feel free to come to my office anytime, or I'll send for you if there's anything I'd like to include in the book."

So I started gathering materials, preparing myself to write the book that I considered a milestone in my life that might project me overnight toward an unpredicted career of a writer. It took me two months before I finally sat down to write.

But before I could do that, I was told to see the president. When I entered his office, I saw two armchairs with a coffee table between with some refreshments on it. Obviously, we were going to have some social chats.

"Sit down," he said. "We're going to have a little talk." We sat down facing each other and started sipping our coffee.

"How's the book getting along?"

I was right. What else was there to talk about except the book? But why the refreshments before us so formally prepared as if there was something to celebrate? Maybe he was just so eager to hear from me that I had started writing it.

So I answered, "I have gathered the materials I need. I'm now preparing the questions I'll have to ask you for your biography. So I'll be asking you for a long interview anytime."

I noticed that his mind was not focused on what I was saying, so I stopped and concentrated on the refreshments before me, starting with my coffee.

His next question surprised me completely. It had nothing to do with the topic on hand. "Do you know a student by this name?" He mentioned her name.

Of course I knew her. She was a very pretty one, who stood out among all her female classmates. "Yes, sir," I replied. "Why do you ask?"

"I'm going to marry her."

I almost choked on my coffee I was sipping.

He watched my reaction, rather amused. Then he said, "You remember what I told you before that, being my biographer, my life is an open book to you? You are the first to know about this."

I was still confoundedly aghast that I did not know what to say.

"Go on, you can say anything to me. I'm prepared for that."

"Why, sir? Why marry her? She is so young, only about twenty. You are seventy-eight—almost eighty!"

"I know that."

"Besides, have you asked yourself why she wants to marry you?"

"I am aware of that, too. Because of my name, which means power and wealth."

"Then why? You are old enough to be her grandfather. She doesn't love you. How could she? She only wants your name and wealth. In the name of God, why do you want to marry her?"

"Look at it this way," he said solemnly, sipping some coffee, as if trying to ease his emotion. "All my life was spent in building this university. The 'indefatigable builder,' as you described me in your article about me. All my energy and passion and all the resources of my being were spent to make my desire a reality. That dedication even surpassed that for my family." He paused for a while and looked around him, as though sweeping in one glance the concrete evidence of his lifetime's achievement.

Then he continued, "So here it is—the biggest university in this part of the world. And here I am, the builder—all spent, weary, and worn out. All prepared and ready to retire." He shook his head sadly as he went on, "Retire to what? My beloved wife has long since died, and all my children are now leading their own lives. So spending my final years without work and activity and with no one beside me to share those years with—it all looks so bleak and empty that I don't even want to think about it."

We both fell silent as we munched some cake and sipped our coffee together. I was thinking of what to say to console him, but all I could tell him was, "It's not the end of the world for people who retire, is it?"

All at once, his eyes shone and his aged face glowed as he answered me, "For me, no. It will not be the end of the world for me. In fact, it will be just another beginning. Why? Do you know what keeps me going? It's the unspoken motto of my life."

"What is that?" I asked.

"You are an English professor, and you should recognize this line: 'To strive, to seek, to find, and not to yield.'"

"Yes, sir, it's from ULYSSES, Tennyson's poem. It's about Ulysses, a mythological hero who did not seek to retire as king in his old age because he wanted 'to drink life to the lees.'"

"Yes, yes, that's it," he said animatedly. "That's what I want to do with this girl I'm going to marry."

I was so touched by his expression that I reached out to touch his hand.

"Thank you," he said with misty eyes. "You see, you don't give up on life because it does not give up on you. If life is wine, one must drink it to the last drop. I think that's what drinking-life-to-the-lees means."

"And this girl you are going to marry is that last drop of wine—right?"

"Right. It is what life reserved for me in my twilight years—life's sweetest gift."

Without batting an eyelash, I asked a very delicate question, "At your age, sir, can you handle this life's-sweetest-gift of yours?"

"I know what you mean," he said unabashedly, and winked at me as he added, "I'll find out."

Those were the three last words of the great man to me—"I'll find out."

I never wrote his book about the history of his university nor his biography. The great founder died not long after he had spent the remaining desire and passion on his "***life's sweetest gift.***"

# 8

# Pleasure and Satisfaction

## Narrative: The Fangs of Pleasure

# Pleasure and Satisfaction

Why the modern man is in constant pursuit of pleasure means only one thing. He wants to escape from something—himself.

He reaches out for something exterior, such as pleasure, to find satisfaction for something interior, such as peace of mind. Thus, pleasure is seeking outside, while satisfaction is finding inside.

But the question is—will man be able to find satisfaction in pleasure? The world provides access to places to accommodate the pleasure-seeking man. Pleasure is where you find it—they are everywhere—for they are places of commerce. But man would pay any price for the pleasure he seeks. Yet, when found, it either satiates or gluts his appetite without satisfying his interior need. Nevertheless, until man finds satisfaction, he won't stop. So he continues to indulge in pleasure—until it becomes a trap. Instead of giving satisfaction, it causes destruction to his finest trait—mastery and control of himself.

For instance, when a man persists to find satisfaction in something like alcohol—or in a certain activity like gambling—pleasure hides its claws and bides its time until it can get hold of him in a vise-like grip that presses him down to irreparable indulgence in excess. And the rest follows—from excess to habit—and ultimately to addiction. Yet, even when brought to such extent as addiction, pleasure doesn't provide the satisfaction he craves for—tranquility and peace of mind.

This shows very clearly that satisfaction is not only elusive, but improbable to find. No matter what, man is restive and goes on and on to find it. It's as if his destiny rests on it, and he has all infinity to find it—and heaven can wait. For after all, heaven is a place of eternal peace of mind, the semblance and foretaste of which man must find first on earth below.

Earthly pleasures are like the siren's song of Greek mythology. So sweet were their songs that the ancient sailors just had to get near the rocks where the sirens sat singing. They knew the danger, but it was impossible to resist. So they went nearer to have the pleasure and fullest satisfaction listening to the siren's song—only to be dashed to their death against the dangerous rocks. In their incontrollable eagerness to get nearer the source of pleasure, and thus be satisfied, they were destroyed instead.

Like the ancient sailors, the modern man loses precaution against the dangers lurking behind the "siren's rocks" of beguiling and beckoning songs of places of pleasure. The world is full of such places—such as movie houses, bars and nightclubs, shopping malls, restaurants, stadiums, casinos, and so on. If a person is not in his home, he is sure to be in these places—day and night. All of them are places of commerce where money flows freely. But man is willing to pay any price—for where else could he have fun—to perhaps find satisfaction? Pleasure and fun go hand in hand. But fun is short-lived. It doesn't last long. When fun stops, pleasure ends—and satisfaction is never found. But the next chance a man has to go back to the source of fun, he grabs it. He goes back to it again and again. In a local casino, for example, the same crowd, with the same faces, are seen over and over again. They come back, even if they lose or go bankrupt. Pleasure is expensive—yet, it cannot buy satisfaction.

Then why does man persist in seeking it? The truth lies within himself, which he does not want to face—loneliness. Modern man is basically lonely. Pleasure, wherever he finds it, fails to make him escape from the loneliness that besets him, which is caused by the boredom and ennui of his own presence. In other words, he cannot run away from his loneliness—except by a temporary respite and escape from it.

So loneliness and pleasure go together, one following the other in an endless cycle of repetitive continuity. Yet, satisfaction, which is the only antidote or panacea to stop such cycle, is nowhere in sight. So go on he must until he finds it. Sometimes it would seem that at last a few steps more and it would be within his reach—only to find out it is only a mirage, common to travelers in the desert. This is an imaginary sight in the distance—an oasis of lush greenery promising water to quench thirst, and food to stave off hunger, and rest for the weary bone. But the more he goes onward in the pursuit of pleasure to find satisfaction, he finds himself going downhill instead in the repetitive monotony of addiction. Peace of mind always seems reachable with the promise of satisfaction that pleasure gives, but actually it is most elusive and unattainable, even from all the pleasures the world can give.

Perhaps, satisfaction is not really meant to be found at all—here on earth.

# The Fangs of Pleasure

This is the true story about Anita, whom I came to know several years ago at a friend's party. Since then we had been in regular contact with each other, either by phone, or by having dinner out or by shopping together, which she loved doing. She was then well over sixty years old, and on old maid.

I knew her then as a very stable person with a good job and a nice apartment where she lived alone. Come payday, my phone would surely ring with her saying, "How about lunch at our good old Chinese restaurant downtown?" And off we would go to her favorite places of pleasure.

I never heard Anita complain about anything. It was as if she was going through a rough sea of life without a single ripple of woes and cares with which others are often beset and burdened with. It is that attitude of hers that life is what you make it. Her simple philosophy of life is—work hard and live well. How? By spending what she was earning on things that give pleasure and fun. To her, there is no sense in counting and keeping money. That was why she enjoyed being with friends wherever they would take her to find pleasure. She even went with them on pleasure cruises, or traveling to various places on long trips.

This went on for a long time until she discovered a different source of pleasure that changed her life entirely. This happened when one of Anita's friends invited her to a casino to celebrate her birthday. Food is always good and sumptuous in casinos. Just play and gamble for a few hours, and then eat all you want, with the least or no money at all to spend on food. Over and above that is the likely chance of winning a lot of money from the slot machines and at the game tables. It was a lucky first night at the casino for Anita. A dollar bet on a slot machine gave her eight hundred dollars. Her excitement knew no bounds. What a place! To win such money like that by just pressing a button? Unbelievable! So the next day, Anita went back there with her casino-going friend. She won another five hundred dollars.

That did it. Anita was caught in the vise-like grip of pleasure in the casino—and that is to have the satisfaction of winning much, much more. Such restiveness is the enemy of peace of mind. She only had to go back again and again to find satisfaction, which was to win more and more. Such compulsion became Anita's obsession—to find pleasure and the satisfaction she craved for at the casino.

However, the grim reality to have more and more money to gamble with loomed its ugly visage for Anita to face and contend with. But she could not easily be taken in and overcome by it. Anita had a good side in her character not to spend beyond her means. That was her bright self, which showed in her smiles and joyful laughter. But the dark forces of life were already at work within her.

A dark force had found the kink in Anita's character, wherein it sank its fangs to suck her lifeblood and cause her utter ruin and destruction. The fangs of pleasure found the very spot to wreak havoc. It was Anita's uncontrollable love to go to casino. All she needed was money to gamble with.

This came to her out of the blue sky, call it providence or unexpected fortune. It was both. An old, rich aunt of hers died without any heir. Her two children already died ahead of her, making Anita her closest relative to inherit her wealth—money, property, jewelry, and all. Anita bought a house in a more respectable neighborhood and deposited in her bank account about half a million dollars.

It was sad to see how sudden wealth could destroy a person the way it did with Anita. She no longer cared for other people, having become selfish and stingy by keeping every-thing for herself—and her pleasure. Where else?

It did not take long for her inherited wealth to be quickly squandered away. She left her job, for her salary was only a pittance compared to what she now had. But it made her lone-lier. No more office mates. No more proximity of apartment dwellers with whom she formerly lived.

Since then, I never saw much of her the way I used to. I heard from a friend working at the bank where Anita deposited her money that she had withdrawn all of it. Her jewels were at the pawn shop—unredeemed.

Even worse was that her house was up for sale. The cost of Anita's pleasure was so high that it resulted in bankruptcy. Instead of giving her satisfaction, it caused her more loneliness and isolation.

The sting of pleasure is in the satisfaction it denies. Also, the emptiness left behind by the venom of its fangs.

# 9

# Selfishness and Generosity

## Narrative: Walk an Extra Mile

# Selfishness and Generosity

W hat is man but his own self! That self is the truth and essence of his being—the totality of what he is—his body and spirit together. This makes him a human being.

All other animals have body, but no spirit. It is what makes man different and superior over all of them. Animals have senses—even intelligence, suited to their nature, which motivate their basic instinct to survive and multiply. But what they lack are man's sensibilities that are induced and governed by his spirit.

All in all, it is man's spirit that dictates and dominates all his motives and actions to live above the level of mere existence. How?

Man's Creator gave man a divine gift besides his soul, which is his spirit. Together with it are its adornments—such as his passions and desires, dreams and ambitions to win as much riches as the world can give—mainly, material wealth. By pursuing such wealth, man's character is tested by its obedience to his Creator's foremost commandment: "Love your neighbor as you love yourself."

That clearly shows that the best test of man's obedience to God's commandment is contained in the word "self"—one's self loving another's self. This is determined by all his personal motives and actions distinguished as his alone by being preceded by the word "self"—such as self-interest, self-respect, self-centeredness, self-defense, self-study, self-service, self-determination, self-sufficiency, and so on.

There is one word, however, that contains the word "self" that goes against God's commandment: "Love thy neighbor as thyself." That word of disobedience is "selfish." It means man loving himself above all others. All he cares for is himself. And all he could get from others by whatever means, he considers his possession. Selfishness knows no limit. It does not take long for greed to take over.

Selfishness and greed sustain each other. One wants to keep what it can grab from another. They go together as an accepted pair as bread and butter, ham and eggs, thread and needle, nail and hammer, and so forth. A man's greed drives him to disregard utterly his neighbor's right to keep his own property without fear of being deprived of it by someone wanting to grab it away from him—legally or illegally.

This happens even in good families. It is common among corrupt government officials in some countries who deprive the people's right to improve their lot. Where dishonesty is, these corruptions thrive with its cohorts—selfishness and greed.

Be that as it may, there is the right side of man where his spirit lies, unsullied by greed and selfishness. That is his generosity. It is giving for the sake of giving without counting the cost, nor expecting something in return. It is a pure act of love, because it is giving more than what is asked for.

Generosity is kindness without measure because sometimes it entails sacrifice. The Biblical "widow's mite" is the perfect example of generosity. A poor widow gave two of her three coins to church, keeping only one for herself and her child. It is giving with sacrifice, which in simple terms is giving with love. This is generosity.

What better and higher generosity can man show than the sacrifice of giving his very life for all his neighbors; by offering it to fight for his country in times of war? Humanity is blessed despite man's greed and selfishness—all because deep in his heart is the willingness to sacrifice his life, if need be, for his country.

This is seen and proven from the ancient times to the present. It is true that greed and selfishness are as old as the history of mankind itself. But so is generosity, which is seen in the ever-happening wars where man's life is sacrificed at the altar of love.

Such altar lies deep in the spirit of humanity itself—and found in every man's being and self.

# Walk an Extra Mile

I am ninety-one years old. They were years and years full of life's experiences, studded with countless people I had met and encountered, most of whom I don't remember anymore. Only those who have left indelible impressions in my memory because of what they had done or said that caught my attention and interests I can now recall.

They all fall under the common category of mankind's opposites: such as the beautiful and the ugly, the rich and the poor, the high and the lowly, the honest and the corrupt, the saint and the sinner, and so forth. Indeed, life is an open book about people who reveal their true selves while interacting among themselves in the endless drama of human situations.

Strangely, one remembers a total stranger more than a close friend or relative—like someone he met at a bus stop, or a co-passenger in a plane; or someone he had a few words with at a shopping mall, market, church, theater, and so on. Insignificant though they seem, man's memory retains them. Why? Because they impart knowledge and understanding of people, in the uniqueness of each one as a human being.

That was how I learned—the dramatist that I am—that one should not judge a person by his appearance. A rich man is a miser because of his selfishness, just as a poor man is like a philanthropist because of his generosity. A beautiful woman is ugly because she is mean, just as an ugly one is beautiful because she is kind and loving. A person who is always inside the church mumbling his prayers is as truly religious and God-loving as a man out in the streets with always a helping hand for the helpless and needy.

Those are the varied kinds of people who compose the vast spectrum of humanity. Their common trait hovers between kindness and generosity on the one hand, and selfishness and greed on the other. In that light, how many are saints compared to sinners? Hardly one against a thousand. It is because more often than not, selfishness and greed take the upper hand.

I have come across some persons I'll never forget because they possess all these traits within themselves, both the good and the bad. But more outstanding is the bad trait because of selfishness and greed that they hide beneath the veil of good. For instance, I have a friend who enjoys my company, so she invites me, now and then, for dinner at her big house where she lives alone. Being a rich woman, she had several servants, including a housekeeper and a chauffeur in her household. What impressed me most is that her table was always full of delicious dishes fit for several guests. But what disturbed me most during my visits was what she did after eating. One of her maids would come near her carrying a plastic bag into which my friend would dump all the uneaten food, even the almost untouched ones, like garbage.

It disturbed me a lot watching her do what, because to me, was terribly wrong and despicable—throwing away good, God-given food like garbage. But I just kept my mouth shut because it was none of my business to meddle with the household practice of anyone. But unable to hold my tongue any longer, I finally asked her, "Why throw away all that delicious food? Why don't you just give it to your servants? I'm sure they'll love and enjoy eating it."

"They have their own food," she replied casually. Then she added, "In my household, servants do not eat what their masters eat."

That remark left me speechless for a few moments because I didn't know what to say. What a revelation of her character! Is it selfishness? No—something worse than that. It was "man's inhumanity to man" in another guise or garb. To treat others, no matter how lowly, unfit to eat what their masters, even their dogs, eat.

I also know someone who is selfish in another way. She was selfish to herself. She would cook one chicken, and that would serve as her food for several days—even for as long as a week. One piece every meal—and that's it.

How about a man I knew very well (a rich uncle of mine) whose selfishness has no description. He travelled abroad a lot, and so he was not in his home often. But before going away, he would have the tires of all his cars removed, to be sure that none of his relatives or servants could drive them, even if they did find the car keys where he hid them.

What about the multimillionaire I heard about whose self-ishness is so singular and unique that it does not alienate at all anyone of his friends who love him more instead? Why? Because he often invites them to expensive restaurants and enjoys watching them eating to their heart's desire—splurging without counting the cost.

One of them finally asked him, "Why do you do this all the time? Why don't we sometimes do "Dutch treat," paying for each one's order? Or better still, why don't you let us invite you instead and be our guest?"

"Don't do that," he answered. "I'm not doing it just because you're my friends. I'm doing it for myself, too,"

"What do you mean doing it for yourself?"

The rich man replied, "It's because of this problem of mine. I don't know how to spend all my millions in my lifetime."

His answer hit the crux of the matter about selfishness. One immutable fact and truth about lifetime is that no one ever knows when it's going to end—perhaps a few weeks, months, or years. It might even be the very same day or night when he is thinking about it. More significantly, one cannot carry his riches with him beyond his lifetime.

But to think of spending his riches for himself alone is self-ishness in its lowest degree and ugliest form. It is greed, too, for it compliments selfishness by keeping for one's self what should go to others in the name of charity.

Such is shown by a family of five in our community. How the four hated their eldest brother! Why? It was because they inherited millions of pesos from their deceased father. By some legal machinations their brother made himself the one in charge of such wealth to distribute equally among the five of them. What he gave to them was very much lower than what he kept for himself. It was his selfishness and greed that kindled their rage and hate that followed him to his grave.

Generosity draws people. Selfishness and greed alienate. Yet there is not much of material wealth involved with generosity. It is more of the giving of one's self to help another. It falls under the category of charity, which is the divine term of love for others.

A poor man is generous, not just because of the amount of money he gives, but because of his heart that goes with it. I don't remember any day when I was a youngster when there was no visitor, friend, or relative coming at home to eat with us. My mother always had some food prepared for them. Some relatives, together with their family, would even stay at home for several days, even weeks. My parents always accommodated them gladly in our humble home. Such generosity is uncommon nowadays. I, for one, would find it hard to do what my parents easily did.

There is a saying, "Money is the root of all evil." What is the root? Selfishness and greed—plain and simple. And what does "all evil" mean? It is the diabolical means by which the devil draws many to him through avarice, envy, stealing, and coveting.

There is also a famous phrase "Walking an extra mile" for a friend. It simply implies giving more of one's self to help another out of love. Such is called "generosity."

What blessedness it is for one who walks that extra mile!

# 10

# The Gift and the Giver

## Narrative: Better Late Than Never

# The Gift and the Giver

It takes two to love—the lover and the loved; just as it also takes two for gift-giving—the giver and the receiver. Usually in most cases, the lover and the giver are the same person; as are the loved one and the receiver. This is a simple fact and truth upon which the splendor of human relationship rests. This is done by the act of sharing.

Sharing what? Of course what a person has—for how can he share with someone something he does not have? The love one gives to another comes from within him—from the very roots and fibers of his being. Whereas the gift he offers to someone is acquired or bought from extraneous sources outside of himself.

In these modern times, gifts are usually bought from stores and shops. There are even gift shops for the purpose of having items appropriate for the one to whom it is intended to be given. Thus, it is not appropriate at all to give a box of chocolates to someone with diabetes; or a beautiful hair pin and comb to a woman almost bald. Nor is it nice, but rather mean, to give an armpit deodorant to someone reeking with armpit odor. That would help him, but it is insulting. Neither is it appropriate and kind to give a choker necklace to a woman with a short, lumpy neck, for it would serve to emphasize her physical defect, or choke her as well. In other words, a gift should be carefully chosen to fit the needs, interests, and looks of the person it is given to.

Giving a book is considered the most appropriate gift; but that depends on the taste of the reader. A book of poetry would not suit the taste of someone who is science-minded. Nor would a jazz or rock music lover enjoy listening to a tape of operas.

The right and appropriate gift is timeless. The giver may have faded away with time from one's memory, but his gift remains to remember him by. Giving gifts is known to have started from the beginning of time. Life itself is a gift to man by his Creator—and together with it are all the means of support he needs to sustain him while alive—such as food, clothing, and shelter.

Thus, the "right to have" is given to man because he needs others to live with—so sharing is an absolute necessity for men to live together and multiply. It could be said, therefore, that giving and sharing serve as the lifeblood of humanity. But it should flow out of the goodness of man's heart to make it valuable and lasting. To make it so, appropriateness should be observed by the giver in choosing it so that the receiver can appreciate it with all his heart.

The best example of gift-giving is beautifully shown in the short story, "The Gift of the Magi" by the American author, O. Henry. It is about a husband and wife who are so poor that they could not even afford to buy a Christmas gift for each other. They don't have any value they could sell—except each's valuable possession he and she would never think of parting with—the husband's precious watch, and the wife's lovely, long hair, which her husband loved about her so much. Come Christmas Day, both were smiling happily, because they each were holding a gift for the other! They didn't even pause to think how on earth they could buy such gifts. Surprised and excited, each one hastily opened his and her beautifully wrapped gift. Lo and behold! Both were open-mouthed and transfixed as they stared at their gifts—a gold chain for the husband's watch; and a beautiful comb and ornament for the wife's lovely hair. Husband and wife sold their most precious and only material possession to buy a Christmas gift for each other. In the name of man's gift-giving, which is more precious and valuable—the gift or the giver?

Both gifts are appropriate, for they are meant to make beautiful each one's dearest possession. Their highest value, however, comes from a sacrifice with which husband and wife lavished on the item they bought to delight each other—then wrapping them up in the ribboned package full of love for each other.

Both gifts transcend the costliest value of anything the world could give that would make them shine brightly with spiritual value that renders to both the gift and the giver eternal blessedness.

Humanity's most valuable lesson on gift-giving concerning both gift and giver is most eloquently expressed—verbally and spiritually in James Russell Lowell's long narrative poem—"The Vision of Sir Launfal" in his short line—"For the gift without the giver is bare." This poetic line needs deep contemplation about human and spiritual values of gift-giving.

The poem is about one of King Arthur's knights of the Round Table who left Camelot to seek in faraway places the object of his soul's quest for the "Holy Grail." It is the spiritual search through man's adventures in life for the symbolic or material manifestation of God's gift to man—wherever he may find it. His quest requires the finest qualities of chivalric courage and bravery to find the "Holy Grail" in whatever form or venture it would show itself. Clad in his shining armor, riding on his beautiful horse, Sir Launfal passed through the bridge leading him away from Camelot toward the world's awaiting adventures ahead.

At the foot of the bridge sat an old bedraggled beggar with his thin, wrinkled hand outstretched for alms from the passing knight. Upon seeing the beggar, Sir Launfal dipped his hand inside his pocket for money. Finding some coins, he tossed some of it to the beggar without even a single glance at the poor man picking up the coins in the dust.

Time passed—a week, a month, a few years—and Sir Launfal encountered all kinds of adventures for his quest to find the Holy Grail. He helped the helpless; rescued maidens in distress; saved men from their enemies, slaying dragons and monsters. He gladdened the hearts of the unfortunates by the shining example of a magnificent knight who cared for them.

But poor Sir Launfal, he never saw the least sign of the Holy Grail throughout all his adventures. Already, he felt too tired to go on. He had to go back home to Camelot—empty-handed, though he was a dismal figure.

He'd be home soon. With a sad smile he slowed down his horse to cross the bridge. With a heavy heart he looked at Camelot ahead, as he thought of his fruitless search. What a sad tale to relate to the knights waiting for him at the Round Table. What would they think of him? How undeservedly he must be of the Lord's favor who denied him of even a glimpse of the Holy Grail! His heart ached: what more could he have done for Him?

At the foot of the bridge to Camelot, he saw the same old beggar sitting with his hand outstretched for alms—the only kind of gift to ask from a passerby that would buy him a piece of bread to feed his hunger. Though too tired and weary, Sir Launfal paused awhile to dip his hand in his pocket for any coin left. Something must have touched his heart at the sight of the old man bent and stooped by poverty to beg for alms.

It was at that moment when the knight realized the truth about himself. He recognized his own poverty! He, the giver of a paltry coin to feed the beggar's hungry mouth, was the receiver of the coin of mercy from above to feed his hungry son! And what he was begging for was just the mere sight of the Holy Grail!

Thereupon, the beggar raised his bowed head to look at the knight. Instantly, above his head shone the dazzling brightness of heavenly light. In the midst of that light was a chalice-like receptacle. The Holy Grail!

Shining in golden splendor, it was the holy chalice that Jesus Christ drank from during the Last Supper. At last, he was gazing at the most sought Christian relic in the world. And it was just right there within his very reach!

Who is this beggar in our world above whose head sparkles the grandest vision of all—as the vision of Sir Launfal? Who was this person who had been sitting there always at the foot of the bridge? Why sit at the bridge of all places? Could it mean that man has his own bridge to cross between life and eternity in the quest of his own Holy Grail? And just right for him to pass by is a beggar with his perennial outstretched hand to any passerby for alms—the mere pittance of something one has to share out of mercy or love—with one who needs it. It is only then that the giver and the receiver become one—upon whom the Holy Grail shines. Not above his head, but right within himself—in his own soul.

And all it takes is a gift shared. What kind of gift is it? This is aptly and beautifully expressed in James Russell Lowell's immortal lines in the poem "The Vision of Sir Launfal." Quote:

Not what we give, but what we share,—
For the gift without the giver is bare;
Who gives himself with his alms feeds three,—
Himself, his hungering neighbor, and me.

# Better Late Than Never

In the small confines of a classroom where learning takes place, humanity's best exchanges of ideas and reactions in a group takes place. It is true that students learn from the teacher; but it is just as true that a teacher learns from his students. As a teacher for thirty-four years of my life, I can say that the essence of teaching is learning gained from those who are taught. Their reactions give meaning and insight into the profound truth in the knowledge imparted to them within the classroom.

Humanity unfolds itself within the microcosmic world of a classroom where the eternal activity of teaching and learning by mankind goes on. Such activity is mainly about interactions of human beings confronted by the necessities and vicissitudes of life as imparted in the subject taught.

This is most true in the teaching of Literature. It offers most to man's thirst for knowledge about humanity. It is said that "literature is the mirror of life." In other words, it is congealed humanity itself expressed by the best thoughts and writings of the best minds of all ages.

It usually happens in the teaching of Literature that profound truths about life arise, which need to be focused on. This happened once in my class when the poem being discussed was James Russell Lowell's "The Vision of Sir Launfal"—with the line "the gift without the giver is bare."

I paused for a while to make clear that the line's deep meaning by relating it to my students' own experiences. I asked them, "What is the gift most precious to you—and do you remember its giver?" They had fun exchanging tales about their respective gifts, and I enjoyed listening to them—until someone asked me, "How about you, Ma'am? What is your most precious gift?"

I didn't answer the question because it was rather personal and confidential. Instead, I told him, "I remember until now the gift I never received in my whole life."

All of them remained silent as they waited for me to explain what I just said.

So I started, "You see, I was more of an outdoor child. I was always out playing with our neighbors' children like me; or climbing trees; chasing and catching small crabs at the riverbank near our house; or catching dragon flies. So nobody ever thought of giving me a doll to play with. But I remember someone who gave me a kitten for my pet. It served as a doll nobody gave me. That is what I mean about a gift I never received in my entire life."

When I dismissed the class, a male student remained behind to tell me something he didn't want his classmates to hear. What he said touched my heart.

"Ma'am, I want to give you a gift. My father raises cattle. He gave me a calf as a pet. May I give it to you? Instead of your pet kitten before, I'm now giving you my calf."

"Why?" was all I could say.

"It's my gift to you for all that you have taught us, which I shall remember always."

I groped for words to thank him. "How very kind and thoughtful of you. Thank you so much. But I cannot accept it. You see, I live in an apartment without a yard with grass to raise and feed a calf." I wanted to embrace my student, but all I could say was, "I shall always remember you and your gift which I cannot accept—your calf."

When I met that class the next day, there was a wrapped box on my table. I looked at my class; everyone was watching me. I sat down before opening the box. Inside it was a doll!

I took it out of the box with surprise and delight—held and gazed at it almost reverently. On the doll's dress was a pinned note that reads: "It's better late than never." There was no name of the giver.

My first doll—a gift in my late years from someone I never came to know. In my heart, I then wanted to add a line of my own to James Russell Lowell's poetic line—"The gift without the giver is bare."

My line is—"The gift from an unknown giver is rare."

# 11

# Looking and Seeing

## Narrative: Blossoms in the Crack

"What is a rose without its thorns?"

# Looking and Seeing

"If eyes are made for seeing
Then beauty is its own excuse for being"

These are famous lines from "The Rhodora," from America's well-known author and poet, Ralph Waldo Emerson. In its brevity lies the unfathomable depth revealing the relationship between beauty and man's eyes.

Both are divine gifts. One could not have been created without the other. However, man's eyes could only be driven if they fulfill their purpose—which is for seeing. To be able to see beauty and truth together in an ordinary thing such as a wayside flower is what gives man his human wisdom.

Man's eyes are made for seeing—yes. But they have to look first so as to behold. From beholding follows seeing—and only then is the sole purpose of man's eyes fulfilled, making them a divine gift. So closely are looking and seeing linked to each other that they can even happen simultaneously. But the distance between them could not be traversed nor measured by time. Man looks at concrete and tangible realities. Seeing penetrates into the abstract and intangible significance of such realities. Why so? Because the soul of man stands between his looking and seeing. It is his soul that makes him see the truth of things concealed under the layers of ordinariness.

If seeing can penetrate into the truth about things, looking can operate in the opposite way. It can drive his thoughts away from truth. How? By thrusting the physical qualities of a person or thing into his attention so it could not dig deeper into concealed truths that seeing might reveal.

Man's looking has many handmaidens, so to speak, which serve to divert his eyes from seeing—such as glancing, staring, viewing, peering, ogling, glaring—all of them having to do with sight. By sight is meant man's instant attention to physical and exterior qualities—such as the shape and form of a woman's body and legs, the contour of her face, the color of her skin—either black or white, the measurement of her waistline and bust, her white and even teeth and others—all of which describe her outer appearance.

If the man's eyes don't like what they're looking at, they move to other things around him, so profuse and innumerable they are, that man has no time to let his eyes see whatever truth lies beneath the outer layers of appearance. Besides, man is always on the go, and in a hurry. Seeing takes time—more so, if it prolongs itself to divine or meditates on what he sees.

So what does he care about "To see a World in a Grain of Sand, and a Heaven in a Wild Flower"—as the poet, William Blake, wrote in his "Auguries of Innocence." The profound idea behind such lines are so infinitely remote from the limited expanse of man's thoughts—so how can he relate such profundity with the ordinary reality of his daily life?

That is precisely why man has eyes for seeing to understand the truth beneath such lines. This was what made Joyce Kilmer see in his "Trees." Quote:

A tree whose hungry mouth is prest
Against the earth's sweet flowing breast;
A tree that looks at God all day,
And lifts her leafy arms to pray;

It also was how William Wordsworth saw in his recluse sister, like "a violet by a mossy stone, half-hidden from the eye."

In a grander view of what seeing truly is, Wordsworth gave us his poem about the daffodils, "I wandered Lonely as a Cloud." While walking one day along a field—he saw at a glance "a host of ten thousand golden daffodils, tossing their heads in sprightly dance." The image of those daffodils never left his mind—as he wrote in the poem's last lines. Quote:

> For oft, when on my couch I lie
> In vacant or pensive mood,
> They flash upon the inward eye
> Which is the bliss of solitude;

That "inward eye" is man's imagination that instantly flashes the image produced by his seeing eyes. The mind stores such images in man's memory that he could open up anytime like an album during such moments when he is in "a vacant or pensive mood."

Beauty surrounds man wherever he turns. Nature produces and offers that for him to see—but only if he delves deep into his soul wherein lies the divine mystery of beauty and truth.

And there it is, beckoning man to see Nature's beauty surrounding him—from the majestic mountains and the lowly valleys with their towering trees and tiny plants; from the mighty seas and gurgling brooks teeming with swimming creatures of all shapes and colors; from the lofty skies and air shining with the brilliance of stars and the brightness of flying birds.

To sum it all, such magnificence of earth and sky was created for man to see "the beauty that is its own excuse for being"—the poetic lines that very briefly, but succinctly, express the language of the soul.

Such language of the soul echoes and reverberates within every moment of his life here on earth—and in heaven for all eternity. The fullness and essence of it all is contained in the last few words of John Keat's immortal poem, "Ode on a Grecian Urn." Quote:

> Beauty is truth, truth beauty,—that is all
> Ye know on earth, and all ye need to know.

# Blossoms in the Crack

This is the story and description of a plant that sprouted out of a small crack in the narrow cement passageway leading to the front door of our house. Its height reaching up to a person's waist, with its thick spreading foliage, makes one wonder about its growth at all. Such wonder is eloquently expressed in a short poem, "Flower in the Crannied Wall" by one of England's best poets, Alfred Tennyson. Quote:

Flower in the crannied wall,
I pluck you out of the crannies,
I hold you here, root and all, in my hand,
Little flower—but if I could understand
What you are, root and all, and all in all,
I should know what God and man is.

It is common to see little plants growing out of crannies or cracks on cement surfaces of roads less trodden by man. He hardly notices them and merely passes them by. Thus he fails to see and wonder about the mystery of life in all creation as revealed by that "little flower in the crannied wall."

So how can man's unseeing eyes wonder at Nature's magnificence rising out unbidden on the earth's surface? Such as the lofty mountains and hills with their towering trees and hanging vines? Or the low valley below whose naked bosom is covered by manifold plants and wayside flowers scattered untended in fields and earth's open surfaces?

Nor can his unseeing eyes perceive beauty in a flock of migrating birds perched atop the surface of a worn-out, dilapidated structure, chirping and singing together, until, with the unified flatter of their little wings, they fly away to resume their flight. Furthermore, can man's unseeing eyes notice with amazed wonder the indescribable beauty of a single butterfly preening in its lovely colors atop the rough, dirty surface of a withered tree stump jutting out, like Nature's sore thumb from muddy ground.

So it is that beauty is where you see it—even in its ugly surroundings. Any kind of adornment can only make it less beautiful and superficial. This is shown by Emerson's Rhodora, whose beauty remains pristine and pure, unsullied as it is, by man's touch and care—giving it its "own excuse for being."

Such is the awesome beauty of the wild plant that grew out of the small crack in the cement passageway leading to our house's front door. Where did it come from? No seed had been planted, nor was there space wide enough for its countless stems and leaves shooting out each day in such profusion to replace the withering ones.

One day, my son, who had pots of flowering plants along that passageway, cut down completely the wild ferns growing out of the crack in the cement floor. The flowerpots of his were expensive, so he gave them very special care. But they were being hidden from view by the prominence of the profusion of the uncared-for wild growth from the narrow cement crack.

To no avail, because though cut down completely, the wild plant grew more abundantly—and as if defying man's devastating act of depriving them of its natural right to life, it grew more kinds of ferns of various leaves and stems, unthought of as possible for such variety to grow together. And the miracle of it all is their growing out of a small cement crack.

The plants in my son's flowerpots have long since died and withered, leaving only their brown, brittle stems sticking out of the pots to remember them by.

How about the wild plants in the cement crack? They are still growing in their leafy abundance, unnourished by man's care; but only by the sun and rain from above.

# 12

# Talking and Speaking
## Narrative: The Sharpest Blade

# Talking and Speaking

Among the five senses of man, which are seeing, hearing, smelling, speaking, and feeling, it is speaking, which has a place among the four freedoms formulated and instituted by freedom-loving people to make democracy work for the common good of the nation and its people.

"Freedom of speech"—these three words contain the meaning and essence of human freedom. Constraints or license imposed on the free expression of man's ideas and ideals serve as the means to subvert the end of his best and noblest intentions and aspirations.

Basically, speech is what links together all man's other senses by giving utterance to what he sees, hears, smells, and feels. However, he does not utter and express any of these to himself. He has to talk or speak to someone else to share with him what he needs to express. The saying, "No man is an island," pertains mostly and fundamentally on man's need to speak and talk to someone else—a need as basic as food for man's survival.

In humanity's incessant verbal exchanges, what do men talk about mostly and speak of all the time? Actually, it's nothing more than the unpredictable fortunes or misfortunes of time that affect their daily living. All these find expression in human speech.

However, talking and speaking, which make up speech, are not easy as it seems. Unlike an animal whose growls speak for all its expressions, man's speech is an art requiring improvement and refinement to be able to express his ideas clearly and effectively—even giving voice to the innuendo of his inmost thoughts.

That is why schools from the grades to colleges have subjects that have to do with speech improvement. The English Department serves as the training ground for such activities. In a university, the English Department is not complete without its Speech Lab, which has all the gadgets, instruments, and equipment for a more sophisticated speech-improvement drills and exercises—from correct pronunciation to intonation.

A writer needs only his pen to create a good speech. But a speaker needs not only a well-written speech to deliver, but, more importantly, is how he delivers his speech. Not in a pompous and artless manner, but rather by connecting directly with his audience by his casual tone of talking or speaking to each listener.

Great speeches have made history and their speakers immortal in mankind's memory from the ancient times to the present. Why so? Because such speeches were eloquently delivered due to simplicity of words combined to contain great thoughts.

The listeners to such speeches themselves were fired up to great actions that made them patriots or heroes. As when Leonidas, king of ancient Sparta who was to protect Athens and the entire Greece from hordes of thousands of Persian invaders, heard what his messenger said about the enemy, "The enemies are so many that their arrows will hide the sun." His retort of a few words changed the course of history, "Good," he said, "we will fight under the shade." His three hundred men helped prevent the thousands upon thousands of Persians from conquering Athens in the famous Battle of Thermopylae.

Equally, when Julius Caesar uttered his three famous phrases: "I came, I saw, I conquered," the whole world practically fell under the yoke of the great Roman Empire. Likewise, the three words: "I shall return" of General Douglas MacArthur gave untold hope and fortitude to the Filipino people during the darkest period of their country's history when the Philippines was captured and occupied by the Japanese forces for four long years during World War II.

Not less immortal and no more heart-shaking were Abraham Lincoln's last few words in his very brief Gettysburg Address: ". . . a government of the people, by the people, and for the people." America's concept of democracy was hammered and nailed in the heart of its people by those few famous words. Again, democracy rang out its compelling tone more inspiringly in Martin Luther King's immortal words: " . . . I have a dream . . ." His voice united all races and colors in America in a bond of nationhood.

This cry for nationhood that reverberated throughout America was further brought to greater heights of resonance by John F. Kennedy's inaugural speech. Some words in that speech congealed into a challenge to "the Land of the free, and the home of the brave." Quote:

"Ask not what your country can do for you,
But what you can do for your country."

Like an instant flame, people throughout the land were fired into action to halt foreign ideologies from spreading—seeking the decline or destruction of democracy. The people's zeal to answer and line up to the challenge imposed upon them by the powerful speeches of their country's great men brought to naught the advancing mighty forces of democracy's enemies.

Thus, America became the bastion of democracy in the entire world, taking other freedom-loving nations under its banner. This banner speaks of superiority that had sprung out of the nation's great speeches delivered on a tone of casual talking and speaking that found its way easily and deeply in the hearts of listeners.

No less important than the speeches of great men are the common talking and speaking among people in their daily activities. Said or uttered in the tone of casual verbal exchange, talking and speaking could produce various results. A word said in a malicious tone could wreck a person's honor or reputation; whereas, a word commending what's best in a person would tell much of the speaker's goodness.

So what is it in man's speech that gave its place among the four freedoms? It's nothing more than the talking and speaking that connect the speaker to his listeners. Only then could they move together toward a common good for all—and, ultimately work together for a better world.

# The Sharpest Blade

The sharpness of a knife is what gives it its worth. To be able to cut a given material into desired size or shape to suit man's purpose is its function. To keep its sharpness, a knife has to be honed now and then. A sharp knife should cut neatly so as not to leave jagged edges and rough surfaces. Inanimate as it is, a sharp knife is of good use to man. But also, it can be used to do the worst of harm. It depends, therefore, on how man uses it.

What animate object could compare to a knife whose sharpness could either be good or bad according to man's use of it? "Cutting a man down to his size" is a common expression that means keeping a man mindful of his inferior personality and possessions. How is that done? What does man use to do it? Not with his nails or teeth, the only sharp parts of his body. What in his body has the sharpness of a knife to "cut a man down to his size"?

A great wonder. Such a feat requiring physical strength is done swiftly and incisively by a mere movement of a fleshy protuberance inside a man's mouth—his tongue. Small as it is, being merely a piece of flesh or muscle—it has the power of a thousand sharp knives to do either good or harm, according to how a man wishes to use it. It can even be regarded as God's instrument in man to speak of love, or it could be the devil's tool that man uses to spit out hate. Could it then be right to assume that in man's tongue lies his salvation—or perdition? To answer that, consider man's delight when he is doing his best pastime—gossiping. While he's at it, a man's tongue, heedlessly and wantonly, wags without restraint—tearing to shreds a man's good name and reputation. Especially if the gossip pertains to a man well-known and popular—as if by gossiping about him would reduce him to be just like anyone, vulnerable to human faults and weaknesses. This makes the gossipers feel good about themselves.

But what makes gossip really bad is that it is not based on facts or truth. More or less, it is merely rumor about a person's private affairs. Man's good sense tells him that—that's why most gossipers don't feel happy about what they're doing—maligning another person who has no chance to protect himself from the sharp stabs inflicted at his back. By what? The limp flesh of a wagging tongue that can stab with the deadly effect of a sharp knife.

Virtually nothing could compare with the human tongue as the sharpest blade. It works nastily in gossip; it is deadly in slander. If gossip throws dirt on a person's good name, slander pours poison on it. Such poison is without antidote because slander once flung cannot be entirely retrieved. The dark shadow of slander follows its poor victim wherever he goes because it had been contrived vindictively and with malevolence to destroy a person's name beyond repair by time itself.

Slander, by itself, is a crime because of its intention, which is tantamount to killing a man's honor and good name upon which his life thrives. It uses the tongue to carry and inflict its deadly intent through false-spoken words and statements to destroy and wreck a person's honor and respectable name.

Slander can be done slyly and subtly by the cleverness of the tongue as used and commanded by the malicious mind. Or it can be blurted cruelly by the tongue that can say crisp, accusing words as easily as it can sing praises. In other words, the sharpest blade, which is man's tongue, can destroy or praise without compunction. It all depends on how man wishes to use it. To speak about love, here and beyond, could mean his salvation, but to spew anger and hate are the warning notes of perdition.

# 13

# Aloneness and Loneliness

## Narrative: Ring Me Up—If . . .

# Aloneness and Loneliness

This is the age of condominiums. Each city in America, as in those of other modern countries, has its own share of these tall buildings, many stories high, to accommodate its ever-growing population. They are seen as common landmarks in cities of the modern world.

Who are the tenants? Mostly loners who get away from their homes and relatives to have their own privacy. Comprising the group are young people who move out of their domination—in order to be on their own. Usually, they take in live-in partners; in most cases, lovers.

Society no longer frowns on this group, on question of morality. To be compatible in togetherness is what matters most to these young people—a necessary factor to make them consider marriage later on. They could be considered as the new urban segment of modern society that emerged from the rise of condominiums.

A number of a city's condos are owned and run by the government, intended to help its low-income citizens. Most of them are senior citizens who are on welfare assistance from the government for their financial needs, including their very low rental payment. Practically, the government even pays their rent.

I used to frequent one such condominium to visit a friend residing there. It is virtually a melting pot of different cultures, customs, languages, religions, etc. Most of its tenants are immigrants from China, Philippines, Vietnam, India—others from far-away Russia and Africa. They live under the same roof, so to speak, but one hardly knows nor speaks with his next-door neighbor who is only a few steps away from his own door. In other words, they are strangers to one another, sharing nothing of themselves even with their close neighbors.

Only one thing they have in common—aloneness. And with it, its natural consequence. Loneliness.

# Ring Me Up—If . . .

Her name was Sonia—single and fifty-three years old when this story about her happened. Though not yet a senior citizen, she was considered as one having been accepted in the city's Center for Filipino senior citizens, most of whom were over sixty.

I was working then as the Social Coordinator of the Center, whose duty was to arrange the social activities for each day of the week. The most-awaited day was Tuesday—the dance-party day. Delicious dishes and delicacies were brought by the members themselves for their lavish party. Live-dance music was provided by a three-member combo-band.

What a day Tuesday always was! Even with their knees creaking, nobody stopped dancing throughout the afternoon. Sonia was a favorite among the old guys, for she was a good dancer. Besides, she simply loved "my old boyfriends" as she called them. She never missed a day being with them at the Center.

One day, she came to my office with a box of chocolates, which she handed to me.

"What's this for?" I asked. "It's not my birthday."

"It is to thank you," she replied.

"Thank me? For what?"

"For making me happy."

"Happy? What do you mean?"

She sat down and was quiet for a while, then said with tears glistening in her eyes, "I don't know what to do with my life if I don't come here." Then added, "Every day."

I didn't say anything to allow her to say more. She didn't.

So I did. "Where do you live?" I asked.

"In a condo downtown."

"With whom?" I kept the conversation going because I felt she needed to talk to someone.

"I live alone."

"Alone? No relatives?"

"A sister." She frowned slightly before adding, "But we hardly see each other."

"Why?" I asked curiously.

"I don't like her husband." Her frown deepened.

I stopped there. I didn't want to pry into personal affairs. I waited for her to say more or to leave.

Sonia stood up but hesitated to leave. As she faced me, I saw tears glistening in her eyes. I remained silent. Finally, she started to speak again.

"May I tell you something?" I just nodded. She continued, "Didn't I tell you that I wouldn't know what to do with my life if I can't come here every day? That's true. I'd rather die if that happened."

"Then come here every day. You know you're always welcome here. Everyone loves you here. Especially your old boyfriends," I said to make her smile.

She smiled wryly. "I wish I could"

"Why, what's stopping you?"

"My legs," she replied. "My knees hurt. I think its arthritis." Then with a very sad voice she added, "What's the use of living if I cannot dance?"

Before I could answer she blurted out, "Besides, I notice that I easily get tired now." She laid a hand on her chest as she said, "It must be my heart."

"Why don't you see a doctor?"

"I did. He advised surgery for my knees."

"How about your heart? What did he say?"

Sonia brushed the question aside. "I don't want to think about it," was all she said, then sighing heavily, which sounded like a moan of deep pain, she cried out, "I'm so alone!"

Her tears were now streaking down her cheeks. I handed her a tissue paper to wipe them, not saying anything.

A few moments of silence followed because I did not know what to say to this woman before me. A very lonely woman.

Then finally I thought of something to say to her to make her feel better. "Look, Sonia, perhaps we can manage to arrange this matter. Just call me up if you want to come here. I'll try to find someone to fetch you from your condo. If you need a wheelchair, I'll try to find one for you."

"It's too much bother," she answered.

"No sweat. Just call me up after a few days. By then I shall have arranged everything. First, a wheelchair and then someone to fetch you. I cannot promise to have you fetched every day, but we'll do our best."

She came to me, took my hand, and held it tight. "Thank you, you're so kind." Then with a forced smile, she said something I'll never forget.

"I won't call you up. I know you are a very busy person. I hate to bother you. But if you don't see me around here, just ring me up. I love to hear my phone ringing. At least, someone cares to call me up."

Before I could answer, she squeezed my hand as she said, "Please ring me up—if . . . " She left not finishing whatever she still wanted to say.

Sonia did not come to the Center for three days. I called up her number. Nobody answered.

The Center's Director and I went to the condominium where Sonia lived. The condo Director himself opened Sonia's door for us.

She was lying face down on the floor beside her telephone table—dead. As I looked at her lifeless on the floor, I remembered her last words to me, "Ring me up—if . . ."

What did she mean?

I think I knew the answer even then. It had to do with me. Could it be that had I rung her up if she didn't show up at the Center, it might have saved her life?

Did she really mean it in her heart that she enjoyed the sound of her phone ringing? Could that have saved her from the crushing loneliness of living alone high up in her condominium? How she must have meant it when she said to me, "I'd rather die if I cannot come here at the Center, and be among you."

"Ring me up—if . . ." What she must have meant was, if she could no longer come to the Center, she'd rather die. It was a cry for help.

The same anguished cry of hers that I shall never forget—the loneliest cry I have ever heard—"I am so alone!"

# 14

## Talk or Perish

### Narrative: May I Use Your Cellphone?

# Talk or Perish

Nowadays, a house without a telephone is unthinkable. So is a person without a cell phone. This he carries with him everywhere he goes—the most essential item in his pocket, or in his bag. It is something that practically he cannot do without. Why so?

Communication governs the world today in all areas of human activity. Modern man cannot be alone. He has to talk to someone or else feel lost or isolated. Thus it is that that the most common sight everywhere is a man holding his cell phone near his mouth, whether he is walking on the street, driving his car, doing his work or playing, up in the air in an airplane, or aboard a ship at sea—anywhere you find him on land, water, and air.

Why has the cell phone risen to such prominence, tiny as it is, in the vast, universal network of modern communication? Simply because it drives silence away. Silence is the vacuum of sound—and modern man cannot thrive in it. Sound is as important to him as the air he breathes; it brings the sign of life as he grapples his way through the paths of daily living. He is a part of it amidst the sound of human traffic everywhere, as in the markets of buying and selling, the various tones and roars of the crowd, blaring music in the air, the incessant grating sound of moving vehicles. Man is born in the world of sound with his cry as he comes out of the silence of his mother's womb as the sound of life itself.

And so it is that man is a part, if not the source, of sounds in this world—over and above all of the sound of his voice talking to someone, at any instant—anywhere he is, anytime.

The collective voice of mankind talking to each other—anywhere, anytime—is the sound of humanity. The cell phone has much to do with this—nowadays. It wards off silence, especially the intrusive silence of man's aloneness in the madhouse of sounds and noise of this world in which he lives.

So talk he must. Talk or perish. Thus is modern man's urgent need for a cell phone—his most constant companion and helper at any instant—wherever he is, anytime.

I never possessed nor carried a cell phone with me. The old fogey that I am, I hardly believed then in its valuable use wherever I am. Talking to someone can wait until I get home and use my good old telephone.

Not until I once found myself in a situation when I had to approach a total stranger, and for the life of me, had to ask him. . . .

# "May I Use Your Cell Phone?"

It was late that December afternoon—and it was growing dark. I just came out of a building downtown where I had an appointment with my doctor. Offices had closed for the day, and most of the workers and employees had already gone home—except for some few like me still waiting for their bus to take them home.

But even those few had gone by the time I came hurrying out of the building to catch my bus. To my dismay, I saw it already leaving. I missed it. It would take another hour for the next one to come. One hour to wait—alone.

Alone in the street? God help me. It was the street downtown that everyone avoids, especially during late hours for fear of being held up or harmed. But I had to wait by the bus stop for my ride. By now, the street was already deserted.

What to do? I was scared. I was hoping, even praying, for a taxicab to pass by. I would take it no matter what it would cost me—just to get home safe. Not even one passed by.

Five minutes. Another five . . . then ten. Good Lord! Another forty minutes. It seemed like eternity. By now, it was completely dark. I prayed. God heard my prayer. A man appeared and stopped by the bus stop where I was. He must be waiting for his bus, too—like me.

Thank God! At least, I was not alone anymore. Then he took something out of his pocket. A cell phone. Just what I needed to call up a taxicab. I watched him talking to someone—his wife maybe—telling her he would be home soon. After a few moments, with the cell phone still in his hand, he was walking away.

"Oh, no! Don't leave me . . ." I must have uttered those words aloud, for he stopped in his tracks. I rushed to his side and held his arm so he could not walk away. He looked at me closely, and I looked at him, too. A young man, twenty-five years or so, clean-shaven. I felt safe near him.

I could not say a word. What would I say to a total stranger whom I was stopping to take another step? An unthinkable, if not preposterous situation. Neither did he say a word, too, as he obviously was sizing me up, on guard against any harm I might do him. I could almost read his thoughts. "Not a young woman with strong legs who would run away with my cell phone as soon as I hand it to her. But an elderly woman? What's she up to?"

It was so awkward. The two of us—total strangers to each other—standing close to each other in that dark street—and not saying anything, both of us. I had to say something to explain the very strange thing I did. But all I could say was, "May I use your cell phone?"

"Why?" he asked bluntly.

"To call up a taxi. I need one very badly. Please don't leave me until I get one, please? You see, I missed my bus. The next one will come about half an hour later. I am afraid to be here alone."

He must have read the fear in my eyes that I could not hide. He smiled and said, "I'll do something better than lend you my cell phone. I'll call up a taxicab for you myself."

He dialed some numbers, then spoke some words. After a moment, he put his cell phone back in his pocket. He turned to me, saying, "Your cab will be here in three minutes. It's just nearby." Then he added, "I'll stay here with you until it arrives."

He remained standing beside me until he said, "Your cab is here. I see it coming."

I found my voice. "How can I ever thank you?"

I was completely taken aback by his answer. "I should be the one to thank you."

"Come again?" I thought I did not hear right.

"I actually did all this for my mother. This should not happen to her—to be in a situation where you're in now." He paused for a moment, before he continued, "You just did something very important for me. I'll have to require my mother to carry a cell phone with her wherever she goes."

Then winking at me, and smiling, he said, "Ma'am, you should be carrying one yourself. It's not always that a good Samaritan will happen to pass by to help you."

"Like you," I replied with my voice almost choking with gratitude.

He opened the cab's door for me and helped me get inside before he said, "Yes, like me." And he grinned.

I'm an old fogey, but unlike myself before, I now have a cell phone in my bag wherever I go. Thanks to a total stranger I encountered one late afternoon in a dark street four years ago. He taught me the importance of such a tiny gadget of communications to anyone in the world where anything can happen.

It assured instant response—even help. Especially the kind of help one needs to make him feel he is not alone.

Anywhere he is. Anytime.

# 15

## Silence Among Many

### Narrative: I Want to Dance With You

# Silence Among Many

Words are the vehicles of speech. To move them, you have to utter them to speak to someone. Speaking leads to concentration, and communication follows. Communication is the exchange of thoughts, ideas, and opinions; of feelings and emotions; teachings and confidences, and so on. Such exchanges establish a bond between the parties speaking to one another. It is this bond that builds human relationships upon which humanity rests.

"No man is an island" is the saying that best explains all this. Man is a social animal. Unlike any other animal, to live together means to speak, converse, and communicate with one another to work for the common good—which means their survival.

To be silent among his own kind amidst the sounds of their voices and activities is to be out of and not a part of the stream of humanity.

Silence of the dumb is one thing. The silence of one who does want to talk is another. Yet, there are many who purposely avoid talking, thus resorting to silence in their daily lives. A common expression goes, "The cat ate his tongue?"

No—not at all. It's just that such a man chooses to be silent and live in a world of his own. Religious people, for instance, choose to leave behind them the noise of the workaday world—to seek the silence of prayer and contemplation in cloisters and monasteries. Sign language is another form silence; so is body language to convey personal messages. Nothing is more silent than the language of the eyes, and gestures that do not need speech.

The question is why choose silence when it is easier and more convenient to speak? Could it be because of one's feeling of inadequacy, such as his inability to express his thoughts? Speech defects and lack of communication skills could cause such feeling. Is it shyness due to inferiority or alienation from his group? Or, is it just plain disinterested and boredom, or just the desire to be left alone?

Or might it be the hesitation to share of one's self, especially his thoughts and feelings, with anyone not worth sharing it with. This makes him an introvert who regards even casual talk as exterior nearness.

But talk he must with others because it is a social compulsion to connect with them to be a part of human groups in society. Otherwise, he will find himself an outsider to be ignored and left behind—and ultimately forgotten.

Man is gifted with speech. Not to make use of it is to fail in the very purpose given him by his Creator. This is to live among many in this world who demand speaking to one another for the good of all.

I am a playwright—a dramatist. To me, silence is worth a thousand words, so to speak. In other words, I find drama in silence. A character with only a few words to say, or not a word at all, could make a major character. Amidst the continuous stir of acting and dialogue, which keeps the play alive and going, a silent character could be a dramatic bombshell. One word he utters could spark the fire of instant attention and reaction from the audience I know. I wrote two plays with such a character—one with only a word to say throughout the play; the other with not a single word to utter. Both were winners in my country's annual national literary contest—its most prestigious recognition for local writers.

That is why I maintain that a silent person in the midst of many makes a very interesting character—not only on stage, but in real life as well. What happens when he breaks his own silence?

One word out of him would open the floodgates of his thoughts—even of his own being. What ensues is the flow of words in the stream of verbal exchanges of men speaking to one another about ways and means to tackle daily problems and needs common to all. Or maybe, just making light conversation like gossiping—also common to all.

In short, man is not meant to spend his years in self-isolation by his silence among many . . . to live in the world where "no man is an island."

However, there are some who do—living in silence as mere bystanders, not as participants in the talks going on around them.

I once had an encounter with two.

# I Want to Dance With You

Five years ago, I underwent an open-heart surgery—a triple as it is called. It took almost three months for me to recover, a month of which was spent at a Rehabilitation Center. Most of the patients there were elderly like me who moved around in wheelchairs. We were nursed and trained to be physically fit—especially to be able to walk normally again, and therefore be up and going to resume our former activities of daily living.

I shared my room at the Rehab with another woman; a thick draw curtain was all that served as a wall between us. During all the weeks that we were together, my roommate and I never talked to each other—not a single word passed between us, as though we were poles apart, with oceans between us, instead of a curtain. I tried once to break the silence by saying "Hi." No response—so I had to keep my mouth shut after that. No talk was the proper thing to do to get along with that sphinxlike roommate of mine.

But I could not ignore it altogether. I wondered why she did not want to talk to me—nor with anyone for that matter—such as the nurses and others who attended to her. What's more, they even ended up scratched or their hair pulled if they so much as got near her to talk to her. She had a fierce temper too, if one tries to break her silence.

"Is she dumb?" I asked myself. No, she was not. I know that for sure. At night when the lights were out, and she was supposed to be sleeping, I often heard her mumbling, even

165

speaking—to herself! She spoke in a language I didn't under-stand. So she must be a foreigner—a European, most likely, by her looks.

At her age (she must then be in her eighties), she still had the traces of a once beautiful woman, with the air of dignity of one belonging to the upper class. Nothing common about her. Uncommon? Yes—and that was her perpetual silence. I was already studying a character—the dramatist that I always am, anywhere.

I tried again to break her silence. If I could only hear that voice of hers! My chance came when she was being pushed out of our room in her wheelchair to a waiting car to be brought home. As she was passing by me, I said, "Goodbye." She smiled a little—but no word.

So that was that. I had other people at the Rehab to talk to anyway—especially at the Physical Therapy Room. It was there where patients like me were given all the exercise needed to make our arms and legs function normally again. There were machines to do that, plus exercises to limber them up.

There were around fifteen of us in that class. One was a man who remained in his wheelchair and was given only exer-cises for his arms, not his legs. I surmised he no longer could use them. So during our leg exercises, he just sat in his wheel-chair watching us. I never heard his voice. He didn't talk nor said anything amidst all the activities going on in that room. As if I had not enough of my silent roommate, here I was again with another one. Like her, he had good looks with his graying hair, plus the air of dignity about him belonging to a leader, not a follower—or that of a boss, not of a mere employee.

During the leg exercises, I had to stand up from my wheel-chair to join the others moving their legs in unison with the accompanying music and the counting of our instructor. "Step forward—one, two, three; backward—one, two, three—on and on. So as not to be bored, I did something else—dance steps instead. I did that when no one was watching—except the man in his wheelchair.

But I didn't care if he was watching me. He didn't talk anyway. But I caught his eye following my every move. I winked at him once while I was doing my dance steps. No reaction. Thereupon, I thought of doing something to illicit even the least reaction from him. I faced him and naughtily wiggled my hips. Nothing happened. He just kept on staring at me—not blankly though, for his eyes revealed that impersonal, meaningless interest of his. Nothing more.

Then came the day I was to leave the Rehab Center to go home. I asked the attendant who was pushing my wheelchair to my son's car, who was waiting for me, to take me to the physical therapy room, for it was my class's exercise day. I had to say goodbye to my classmates and instructors. The silent man in his wheelchair was there in his usual corner. I wheeled myself to him and said, "I hope you get well soon. I think you also want to go home, like me. Goodbye."

I didn't expect him to respond. So how surprised I was when he suddenly moved his hand and grabbed mine and held it in a tight grasp! Then came out his voice at last, crisp and clear, "I want to dance with you."

I didn't know what to say. How could I? The two of us, both in wheelchairs, my hand in his, with no words spoken for some moments. Then I found my voice and said to him, "Tell you what. Let's leave our wheelchairs and go look for a place where we can dance together all night."

The light that flashed in his eyes, when hearing my words, was enough to brighten the room. But no word from him after that. I slowly pulled my hand—still in his tight grasp—and left.

Until now, I still find myself thinking of that encounter of mine with a silent man who gave me such a glow in my memory. What if I stayed longer at the Rehabilitation Center? Most probably there would have been more conversations between us, thus restoring him to his old former self—no longer silent among many.

I learned from my stay at the Rehabilitation Center that silence among the aged could be caused by either of two reasons. One was that of my roommate, whose bitter silence might have been caused by painful memories in her past. The other was the silence of that old man in his wheelchair, whose past years might have been filled with a beautiful someone who probably had long since gone—and left him forever.

I now regard the silence of the aged among many worth pondering on—the dramatist that I am, and always will be.

# 16

# Teaching and Counseling
## Narrative: Thank You for My New Life

# Teaching and Counseling

Teaching is for the mind—counseling is for character. The first deals with knowledge; the other with values and morals. The first is gauged with diplomas and certificates earned by formal education in schools—which is measurable. The other is gauged in the respect and honors other people give him—which is immeasurable.

However, both teaching and counseling are intertwined and inextricable from each other—because the teacher is also a counselor. He deals with students who represent all humanity with its perennial thirst to learn. From the time one is born, he instantly starts learning—first, from his dependency in his mother's breast, to self-help in his later years in the world outside of his mother's care.

The rudiments of knowledge he learns from his first teacher—his mother—such as the alphabet, how to write his name, how to count, and many more. Then he goes to school, and the educators take over.

But there are many other things he learns from his mother, such as respect for authority of parents. This he carries with him later on, as manifested in his respect for his superiors anywhere he finds them—from community to government, in society and workplaces, and in all other places where he associates with people. He thereby becomes an important segment in such social groups—equipped as he is with his knowledge and fine character to contribute to the interests and welfare of all.

With my thirty-four years of teaching, most of which were at a university as an English professor, I gained a wealth of experience not only as a teacher, but as a counselor as well. Students would come to me, even at home—not, for instance, to ask about Shakespeare's famous quotation, "To be or not to be," that expresses Hamlet's predicament—but rather seeking help for their own predicament over some personal problems. They came to me, not as their teacher—but as their counselor.

In schools, especially the university, there are various departments for each particular branch of knowledge: such as the Departments of English, History, Science, Social Sciences, and others. But there is not any single department that has to do with counseling and its relative areas. Even at the College of Education, which turns out teachers, not one subject about counseling per se is given academic importance that would add to the required units for a student to graduate. Yet, out in the teaching field, a teacher usually finds himself often acting as a counselor, too. To catch a student cheating during a test or examination is a common occurrence inside a classroom. Instant counseling is necessary to correct such wrongdoing before it becomes as habit. This should be between the guilty student and the teacher alone—not to counsel him in the presence of others. He is thankful for that because it saves him from embarrassment, which, therefore, makes him open to counseling.

Promptness is another case among students that needed my immediate counseling. I once confronted a student of mine for always coming late to class. As a working student, he reasoned out that his work at the factory made it difficult for him to be on time for my class. I showed him his poor records, due to his tardiness, and told him to remain after the class so I could have a talk with him.

"What kind of work do you have, and where?" I asked him.

"Wrapping candies in a candy factory," he answered.

"I see. Now listen well," I told him. "You have a choice. Ten years from now, where will you be, and what will you be! Perhaps still wrapping candies in a candy factory. Whereas, if you have a college degree, you may, by then, be the boss in that factory of yours, if not the owner someday—who knows? In other words, you will be moving forward away from being merely a low-salaried candy wrapper. That's what you are studying for. Right now, you are not doing well with your studies. You might even fail because of your poor grades. As your teacher, I think you will do much, much better if you stop being late all the time."

He never was late after that talk.

One case I remember quite well until now was about a student of mine who came to visit me in school two years after she graduated just to tell me . . .

# "THANK YOU FOR MY NEW LIFE"

Her name was Perla—a senior student in one of my literature classes when I first met her. She must have been in her early twenties at that time, for she looked more mature than all her other female classmates. Quite attractive, too, being well-dressed and groomed—makeup and all. Pretty? Yes—that was why I noticed her right off when I first met that class.

She always sat in the front row opposite the teacher's platform, facing me directly. She never chatted with her classmates, as they usually do. She just sat quietly until I entered the classroom. Then she was all attention.

Perla was a special student—always with intelligent answers to my questions with thought-provoking questions she usually asked—a sign that she was well-prepared for the day's lesson.

However, I found something rather unusual, even disturbing, about Perla. There were times when she came late, and as she entered the classroom, the male students winked at one another; even making some funny sounds. She ignored it all, not casting a glance at any of them. Then the class became more alive due to her intelligent presence. Recitation became more lively.

Talk about students inspired by a good teacher. I had always been a teacher inspired by a good student—such as Perla. She drew the best out of me as a teacher, for I think I gave better lectures in that class because of her excellent performance as a student. I would even say that her class-mates derived much from my inspired teaching because of her. In other words, they gained more knowledge out of the daily lessons heightened by the intelligent leadership of Perla.

One day, I asked Perla to remain in the classroom after I dismissed the class.

"I asked you to stay with me for a while because I want to congratulate you for your excellent term paper. I am very much impressed. So I decided to give you an excellent grade—not only for your term paper, but for your grade in this literature subject as well. I congratulate you."

"Thank you," was all her response. But she did not make any word after that. I felt that she wanted to say something, but was making up her mind to say it.

So I continued, "In another month, you will be a graduate. You might even graduate with honors. Congratulations."

"Thank you," she said again, but still not adding any word. I watched her closely. No, she was not impassive nor indifferent. Only perplexed about making up her mind to say something, but could not.

So I went on. "Just go on being what you are, and you will go places with your high scholastic records—plus, your fine personality."

To my great surprise, I saw tears welling in her eyes instead of answering me. I merely watched her silently as she drew out a handkerchief from her pocket to wipe her tears. Finally she said, "I am sorry, but I truly am deeply touched by what you just told me."

"What?" I asked.

"When you told me to go on being what I am, and I'll go places."

"What's wrong with that?"

"Nothing wrong. It's I who am wrong—that's what," she simply replied.

It was I who was now perplexed—dumbfounded even. Before I could say anything, she further said, "Perhaps you will understand me better when I said that it's I who am wrong by my male classmates' attitude toward me. Do you notice their snide whispers and gestures directed at me whenever I entered the classroom late?"

"Oh, yes," I replied. "That always made me curious as to why they behaved that way. They didn't do that with their other female classmates."

Then she blurted it out, "Ma'am, I'm a call-girl. Hospitality or escort girl for hire, as they call it. You know what that means?"

"Tell me," I answered simply.

"It means that the work of a hospitality or escort girl includes sex service. I sell my body; sex for money."

I was shocked. She blurted the truth about herself so bluntly, as if finding relief in sharing such a dark truth with me—not even sparing herself of whatever I would think about her. To lose my high regard and respect for her would, to her, be the purging off the dirt and filth of the kind of life she had been living. She thought of it perhaps as the consequence of the wrong she was doing when she said to me, "It's I who am wrong."

She had blurted it all—her fine clothes, her well-groomed hair and makeup, her long polished fingernails—not the looks of the ordinary female college student. But her excellent grades and high scholastic records! These didn't jive with the kind of person she was.

As if reading my thoughts, she opened her mouth to say more—this time everything else about her. "You see, Ma'am, I was the victim of the cruel circumstances of my life. When my parents died, I was left to care for my younger sister. How was I to do that? Not even a house of our own to live in, nor money to take care of our day-to-day needs like food and clothing— what's more, no money at all for our education, which requires a lot for tuition and other school expenses. To work as a sales-girl would not suffice at all for everything we needed. But we had to study—my sister and I. It was the only way we could extricate ourselves from the rut we were in to have a bright future. But how? That was why I became a call girl. I thought then that to be a hospitality-escort girl was all there was to it.

It was a trap—and I fell in it. In the sideline of such a job was easy money—sex for money."

She paused, so I asked, "Are you still in this kind of job until now?"

Perla nodded. "I thought that as soon as I graduate, I could have a better, respectable job; so I had to study and be good at it. It was hard-earned money to have a college degree." She smiled wryly as she repeated, "Hard-earned money."

We remained silent, she was crying again, and I was quietly thinking of what to say to her. Whatever she does now could not undo nor repair what she had done—so irretrievably lost her past is. Her past is a part of her present; her future already tarnished and sullied beyond any hope of ever cleansing it. Right now, as she was crying before me silently, every tear of hers was a cry for remorse.

"Perla, you are a teacher now—an English major at that. Soon you will be applying for a teaching job."

"No, Ma'am. I am afraid."

Afraid? There it was—a confession of the wrong she had done to her life.

"I can understand that. That's too bad, for you will make a very good teacher."

She had already stopped crying and was preparing to leave. "Wait," I said. "Listen to me. Why don't you go abroad and look for a job there? You have credentials. That's what many young professionals like you do. They work abroad for bigger pay."

Perla smiled wryly again as she said, "Go abroad? I don't have any money for my transportation even if there is a job waiting for me there. Besides, there is my sister I just cannot leave her behind. She is in college now, and I have to help her every way I can, so she, too, can have a college degree. So going abroad is not for me." Then squeezing my hand, she stood up to leave. "Goodbye, Ma'am."

She was already at the door when I hastened to say, "Perla, do you pray?"

She looked back and answered, "Yes, Ma'am. I go to church on Sundays."

"Then pray that God will help you."

"She nodded and left. I never saw her again after she graduated. After two years she came back to the university to look for me. I was so surprised to see her. "Perla, what brought you here?"

She didn't look like her old self anymore. I noticed a look of serenity in her face—whatever it was that made her quite different. She's still pretty, but now in a quiet, unobtrusive way.

"I came to say goodbye to you, Ma'am. I'm going abroad."

"Why, that's fine!" I exclaimed. "Tell me about it."

"I'm married now." Before I could say anything she hastened to add, "I'm married to a foreigner more than twice my age—but that's all right because we love each other."

"That's good news, indeed," I said.

"But what about your sister?"

Perla smiled happily again. "She's also getting married, to a fine, young businessman. So it will be all right for me to leave her behind." She paused before continuing, "God really answered my prayers. I promised my husband I'll be a good wife to him. That's what I also promised God for answering my prayers."

"I'm very happy for you," was all I could say.

"So goodbye, Ma'am, my husband is waiting for me outside."

"Goodbye, Perla. Good luck, and may God bless you."

"Thank you, Ma'am. And thank you for my new life." She hugged me, then left.

Until now I still think of those few words she said to me before she left. "Thank you for my new life."

To me, those words of hers become the epitome of what I once was—a good teacher, and a good counselor.

And that is still what I consider myself to be all my life, though I am now retired.

Also, those words of hers made me a better dramatist.

For as long as there are persons, like Perla, who grapple with the grim realities of life as many in the human race do, there will always be drama.

# 17

# Remembering and Reminiscing

# Remembering and Reminiscing

I f life is an open book, a person's age could, more or less, be told by its pages. If she is sweet sixteen, there are many more blank pages waiting to be filled up with the bulk of stories about her life yet to happen. If a person is ninety, there are perhaps a few more pages left—the last chapters culminating the whole drama of his life.

But what is noticeably obvious about one's book of life is that there are pages more often read than the others. In fact, most of those unread pages are already blurred and faded—unlike the frequently read pages that are still bright and clear; they seem to have just been printed right after a memorable experience happened.

But no matter what, time blurs and obliterates one's memory of the past, as he has to move onward toward the beckoning happenings of the future. But some memories, however, persist and refuse to sink into oblivion in the cesspool of dead memories. Why?

It is because a person's mind takes possession of his life's memorable events into its storehouse of memories—for him to reminisce on as the years go by. The winter of discontent turns into springtime of silent joy when man's ruminations of the past become reminiscences of the present.

This explains why an old person is said to live in the past. For instance, if an old woman is sitting alone doing nothing, with a faraway look not seeing anything, it doesn't mean any kind of cessation of her bodily activities. It is during that time that her mind is busy remembering and reminiscing.

She could be doing nothing, as if frozen into a standstill—but why the light in her eyes and the soft smile on her lips? Why the sparks of liveliness in her unmoving, statue-like appearance? She seems to be somewhere, beyond where she is sitting alone in her chair.

Yes, she is somewhere else. Not in the present where her body is, but in the past with her mind caught in the web of nostalgic memories. She is once again reading her book of life, straying longer in some pages, as though delving deeper into the intimate secrets hidden there. She is then reminiscing. How sad and lonely must a person be with an empty storehouse of secret memories to reminisce on!

Come to think of it, isn't that what life is all about? Collecting and storing up memories? Just like a squirrel that stores up nuts in its hole in a tree—then takes them out, one by one, to crack and eat when the need arises.

In a higher and grander scale, isn't that what history is all about? The history of the world and mankind is but a collection of important events and dates. Such collection serves as the foundation upon which humanity rests as it determines its destiny from the lessons of the past.

It is also mankind's ways and means to march into the future with brighter visions gained from the dark, dim memories of unending wars and conflicts between nations. The tragedy of such dark memories of mankind's sufferings and pains is well expressed by England's poet, Matthew Arnold, in the last lines of his poem, "Dover Beach"—quote:

And we are here as on a darkling plain
Swept with confused alarms of struggle and flight,
Where ignorant armies clash by night.

Be that as it may, another English poet, Alfred Lord Tennyson, gave us the antidote to mankind's tragedy of sufferings. It is about man elevating himself from the dark memories of the past to the brighter realities of the present—as expressed in his poem, "Ulysses"—quote:

One equal temper of heroic hearts,
Made weak by time and fate, but strong in will
To strive, to seek, to find, and not to yield.

Great poems such as those cited above serve as memorials of the past, the way monuments and statues of great heroes do. To gaze at the statue of Abraham Lincoln, for instance, is to remember America's history of battles and civil strife that brought in their wake the peace and unity to the nation. Just as the eternal flame in the tomb of the "Unknown Soldier" is the symbolic light to remember all war heroes who gave their lives fighting for their country. The Vietnam Veterans Memorial Wall in Washington, D.C., with the names of all the American soldiers who died in the Vietnam War inscribed in it, is to remind us that they had not died in vain fighting for democracy in other countries torn by conflicting political ideologies. Surely, every American remembers July 4 as he celebrates his own birthday. And, is there any American who does not feel a sentimental tug in his heart when he is singing the mighty national anthem, "The Star Spangled Banner"? Especially when his voice rises in a louder crescendo in the last line:

O'er the land of the free and the home of the brave.

His voice even swells with emotion if during the song, his eyes are cast on the American flag being raised up the flagpole, waving proudly in the air with all its stars, stripes, and bright red, white, and blue colors.

Such moments are at once the sublime memorial of the living memory of a nation through all the centuries of its history. The mind remembers as the heart reminisces in the silence of evoked nationalism. This is true to all people in any country with their respective flags that symbolize and glorify their nation's history.

History books are great reading, not only for the erudite and intellectual, but also for anyone interested on the story of mankind in a world beset by endless occurrences and changes. Literature books mirror all those in the stories of people and characters interacting among themselves in the ceaseless drama of humanity. And what are movies for? To show people how they are like as they reflect on the stories drawn out from the bottomless resources of human drama as told by moving pictures.

Virtually, everything that a man reads or watches is summed up and contained in two words—remembering and reminiscing. Both are lodged in the mind—such a small organ in the human body. Without it, what is the whole body for? What is a human being without a mind with all its lifetime memories?

Such question throw light on what is said about the mind being the last to go when a man is dying. Its memory is life's last hold of the world he knows about—as he is about to enter a totally unknown world. The mind simply refuses to stop functioning to the very end as it remembers life to its last drop.

The mystery about remembering and reminiscing is that they can be transported from the world of realities to the ethereal heights of profound truths beyond the grasp of ordinary thinking. Remembering becomes meditation; then reminiscing transforms into contemplation.

When a man looks at the flag and ponders on it, his mind lingers along the recondite pathways of memory. What does that colored piece of cloth waving proudly in the air mean? Why should a nation's people die for it just to keep it "still there" waving proudly in the air—although torn and tattered in the battlefields of war?

Pondering on such thoughts, the mind transcends from remembering and reminiscing. How much more when it ponders on the cross? Just two beams of wood nailed horizontally and vertically together—but its meaning is ineffable, beyond thought and words. Yet the profundity of the cross lies on the simplicity of its truth. Such truth is about love and redemption of God for sinful man, by dying on the cross.

Mankind's collective meditation and contemplation on the cross in its daily remembering and reminiscing is its own redemption.

Come to think of it . . .